EXTENDED FAMILY

Rafael Reyes-Ruiz

Rafael Reyes-Ruiz
Extended Family

La Pereza Ediciones

© *Rafael Reyes-Ruiz*
Extended Family

Cover image: iStock/IVOOK

© 2024 Lazy Publisher (La Pereza Ediciones, USA)
www.lapereza.net

All rights reserved.
Partial or total reproduction in any way is prohibited, mechanical, photocopied or electronic, without the respective authorization from the publisher.

ISBN: 978-1-6237523-4-7

Design:
Estudio Sagahón / Leonel Sagahón
www.sagahon.com
Maquetación Julián Herrera

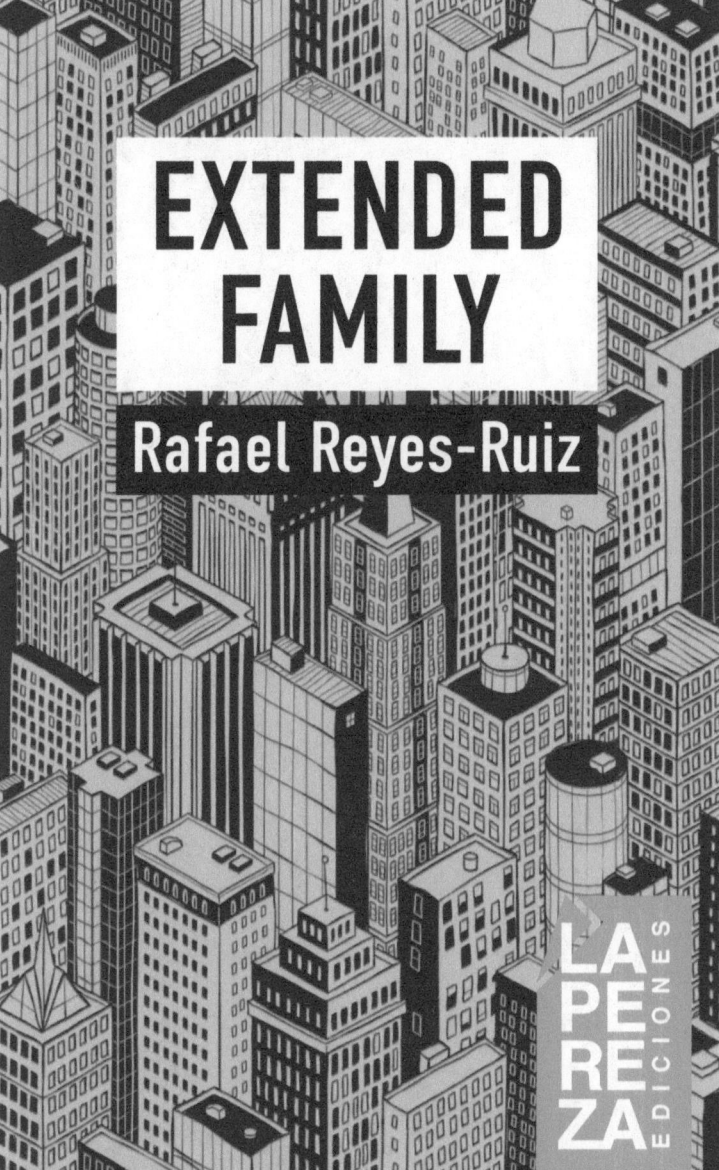

ONE

D'Artagnan was busy with his laptop when I walked into the bar. He didn't notice my presence until I raised my hand in greeting.

"Hello Francisco," he said and gave me a hug from the other side of the bar. "What will you have?"

"A beer would be fine," I replied. He made a face of disapproval and suggested that I keep him company with a double Scotch.

"Your dad would be angry if he saw you with a beer," he pointed out.

I nodded, and, despite myself, I saw Dad lost in the labyrinth of his dementia, in Bogotá.

D'Artagnan perhaps sensed my discomfort. He looked me in the eye, his face showing solidarity, or perhaps solace.

"Have you had any news?"

"I'm told he's the same."

"If you talk to him, tell him I said Hi," he said, rubbing his salt and pepper goatee.

I nodded and took a sip from my glass.

"I found a photo album that you may not have seen," D'Artagnan said, with some emphasis. "It was in a moving box that I had forgotten about. The photos are from the last time your dad was in my bar, in Paris, almost two years ago.

How time passes. I took them, but I never gave him copies. I don't know why, I really don't remember. Those last months were chaotic."

On the first page of –the album were six photos of Dad with several people; I assumed they were regular customers or friends of D'Artagnan. In one of them, Dad was with an older man, as tall as he was, with white hair and a beard. I quickly looked at the other photos –the album had five pages– and I noticed that Dad and the man appeared in almost all of them, along with other people. I was struck by the fact that the older man maintained a somewhat solemn demeanor; he had a formal smile on his face, perhaps it was feigned. It occurred to me that he was someone like me, who hated to be photographed.

As I examined the photos, I noticed, out of the corner of my eye, that D'Artagnan was looking at me with a trace of concern.

"The old man with the beard is Rafael Ruiz, your biological grandfather, your father's father. May he rest in peace," he added in a low voice.

"I don't know what you are talking about."

"I'm sorry, Francisco. I guess your dad didn't tell you."

For a moment I thought that D'Artagnan was joking. It was something he liked to do with friends and some of his clients to make them laugh or as a way to diffuse a tense or embarrassing situation; it was something that Dad used to do too. Maybe that's why they were such good friends. But the flush on his face told me that it wasn't that. I felt a void in my stomach.

"Which biological grandfather?" I asked, perhaps too curtly.

D'Artagnan frowned. "Your dad didn't tell me he hadn't told you."

"Sorry. What you tell me changes a lot of things. Are you sure?"

"Yes, of course. I wouldn't tell you otherwise."

"But how is it possible? Why?"

"I don't know what to tell you, Francisco. I'm really sorry."

I felt a lump in my throat. "Does my Aunt Astrid know?"

"I don't know. I'm truly sorry."

"Why didn't he tell me?" I asked, more to myself than to D'Artagnan, who looked rueful as if *he* had gotten the news.

"The only thing I can tell you is that Gustavo didn't know it either."

"How could he not know?"

"Don't get upset, Francisco."

"I am not upset. I'm confused," I said, and looked D'Artagnan in the eye.

"I'll tell you everything I know. But first, let's toast to your father."

I raised my glass.

"Your dad found out about all this over the phone," D'Artagnan said, a subtle sway in his head. "We were having dinner at my bar in Paris – that was a few days before the night of the photos – and suddenly he got a call from a lawyer friend in Madrid who had news about that old piece of furniture that was stolen from him in Bogotá. An older man had recovered it and claimed that he was his biological father, armed with documents to prove it. Your dad said: 'It can't be. It's a bunch of lies,' and his face turned pale."

"Poor Dad," I said, my gaze on a photo of the two of them. I couldn't help but imagine standing next to them.

"The lawyer told him that the man had documents that proved he was telling the truth. Your dad let the lawyer explain. Then he was silent for a long while and said: 'Yes, now I understand.' When he hung up, his pallor persisted, eyes somewhat glassy. I feared he might faint. But in a matter of moments, his demeanor shifted. In a low and measured tone, he shared that the evidence presented was overwhelming: notarized documents, witnessed signatures on adoption papers, medical certificates, among other compelling proofs."

"His adoption?"

"Yes. Your grandmother Francisca had your father before she married your grandfather Gustavo. According to your father, when your grandmother was sixteen or seventeen, she fell in love with Don Rafael, who at that time was a young craftsman, two or three years older than her. He was doing restorations for the family's antique store. As you can imagine, her parents, your great-grandparents, were against that romance; it was a matter of social class. Even so, they saw each other secretly, and, after a few months, your grandmother became pregnant, but she did not say anything to Don Rafael. Don't ask me why; your dad didn't say anything about it. When your great-grandparents found out, they took her to the Caribbean provinces, to Santa Marta, to your grandmother's cousin's house, so that she could give birth there without anyone in Bogotá finding out about it. Your grandmother's family was very conservative and worried about what people thought. After a few weeks, Don Rafael asked where Francisca was and your great-grandparents told him that she had gone to the United States, to New York, to continue her studies. For some reason that I don't remember – or perhaps your father didn't tell me – Don Rafael left Bogotá; I think he went somewhere south of the country. He didn't come back for six or seven years. When your grandmother married Don Gustavo in Santa Marta, he offered to adopt the child, who was three years old at the time, and gave him his surname."

I wanted to ask D'Artagnan what that man, Rafael Ruiz, was like, what impression he'd had of him, but I held back, perhaps out of loyalty to the memory of my grandfather Gustavo and my grandmother Francisca, who had also passed away. They were my home in Colombia, my roots, what connected me to the past.

"What was he doing in Madrid?" I asked, somewhat irritated. That biological grandfather was nothing to me. He was a stranger who wanted to enter my life with a claim of kinship. Moreover, the *biological* bit seemed absurd and inappropriate to me; it gave it a distant, scientific air. Nothing to do with what I understood it was to be a father or a grandfather.

"Don Rafael was looking for that beautiful piece of antique furniture, the bargueño that was stolen from your dad. Don't ask me why; I don't know. Your father went to Madrid the next day to get back the bargueño and to meet that man ..."

"The bargueño he gave me," I said.

"I guess so. After four or five days, he came back with him to Paris, as his guest. They had become fast friends. They discovered that they had things in common: theosophy, occultism, and all that esoteric stuff your dad likes."

Just then, someone opened the door. The next instant, I felt Ana's hands covering my eyes.

"Anita, do you want a whisky?" I heard.

"Just a finger," she replied in the mocking tone that she used with him, at times a bit condescending, others affectionate, depending on her mood. Ana's moods were even more fickle than mine; the main difference being that her bad moods faded fast, a few hours at the most, while mine could last for days.

"The Uber is coming in four minutes, so chin-chin musketeers," Ana declared and raised her glass. She was wearing her hair pulled back in a bun. It gave her a formal and business-like air, much in contrast to her usual messy wavy mane.

TWO

The party was in a large room with long tables along the walls, on the 10th floor of a building on Sixth Avenue across from Macy's. Through the back windows, you could see the Empire State Building bathed in purple psychedelic colors, or so they seemed to me.

As I walked in, I felt somewhat disoriented. The lights dimmed, and the other side of the room, where I had spotted three or four people—presumably fellow grad students, though I couldn't be sure as they were all wearing costumes—sank into semi-darkness. Ana laughed and took out of her bag the mask and the felt that she bought for me. I put them on, though I didn't want to; I never liked Halloween, never saw the point of it.

"You are *El Zorro*, the real *Zorro*, a good bandit. That's your true nature," Ana said. Then, she put on her mask, which covered her head and half of her face with two little cat ears. "I'm Catwoman," she said and with her hands mimed a cat extending its nails. Ana's gesture made me laugh, though an instant later, I felt a sort of dread, a sense that something wasn't right. Still, I didn't know what it was.

"Welcome," two voices greeted us from the semi-darkness. "King Kong and the Sphinx of the Oracle," Ana ventured, half matter-of-fact and half posing a question, and took my hand, as if she wasn't sure we were before our friends, Ricardo and Natalia, whom I recognized right away, despite their full-body costumes.

After hugs and kisses, Ricardo, who had to take off his gorilla mask, said he wanted to show me his latest acquisition. Intrigued, Ana whispered something into Natalia's ear, and together, they glided toward one of the windows. Ana and Natalia had become good friends throughout the semester. They both had the same academic advisor and took all their classes together. They also shared a passion for classical music and opera, two things I knew very little about. With Ricardo, I found a companion in the disdain for academic orthodoxies and rigid disciplinary boundaries. Despite our shared sentiments, a certain reserve and occasional distance on my part kept us from evolving into close friends. Apart from Natalia and Ricardo, Ana and I were acquainted with the Latin American students from other departments, something that forced me to watch my Spanish. At Stony Brook on Long Island, where I did my undergraduate degree, my friends were all English-speaking; the only foreign students I made friends with were Asians, especially Japanese, through a girlfriend I had for the first two years.

"I'll pour you a shot of mezcal that is out of this world," Ricardo said as we headed towards the semi-darkness from which he and Natalia had come.

"To your health my friend," he declared, and drank his in one go. I took a sip; it had a smooth, smoky flavor. I gulped the rest and felt a tingling in the back of my neck.

"How is your old man?"

"The same, the woman who runs the nursing home tells me."

"Can you believe it?"

"Typical hollow answer," Ricardo replied, sounding ironic.

"Nothing is ever the same."

"It's not possible."

"Did I tell you about the postcard?"

Ricardo shook his head.

My father took some of my things to Bogotá; well, maybe he didn't think they were mine; I wasn't there when he packed. Anyway, when I was visiting him in the nursing home in Bogotá, I noticed that he had a postcard of mine on his nightstand, next to his glasses. It was the Borobudur Buddhist temple complex, in Indonesia, which I kept on my desk in my room. I bought it at a Union Square bookstore years ago, as a curiosity; hardly anyone uses postcards properly these days, they are relics from another era. He was asleep. I stealthily walked to the nightstand and looked at the postcard, something about it had always fascinated me. It is an aerial shot from where you see that the structure is a mandala: a stepped quadrangular shape, within which, at the top, there are bell-shaped stupas, each one housing a Buddha and, at the center of it all, at the highest point, there's the largest stupa, which is empty. At that moment it occurred to me that he had taken the postcard as a kind of memento of me. When I had it in my hands, I noticed that it was worn, and somewhat wrinkled. As if by reflex I turned it over. Dad had written something; I recognized his fluid and graceful handwriting. It was a question: Was I there?

"Was I or was he?" Ricardo asked, his brow furrowed.

"Was he? He didn't remember if he had been there ..."

Ricardo looked me in the eye, shook his head, and poured two drinks.

"Bottoms up," he proposed.

I nodded but only took one sip.

"I'd better go greet the guests," Ricardo said and motioned with raised eyebrows towards the door. Two newly arrived couples were chatting with Ana and Natalia. I couldn't make out who they were. In addition to their costumes –Cinderella, the Wicked Witch, Count Dracula, and a safari hunter– they also wore masks.

I wanted to follow Ricardo through the semi-darkness but held back. Despite myself, the memory of the last day I saw Dad in that horrible house, a couple of months ago, came back. "I'm forgetting my life," he told me when I asked him about the postcard and waved his arms in the air in despair. I felt tears come to my eyes and hugged him. I didn't mean to upset him; I thought he would make a joke out of it like he used to, even when his illness started. I didn't know what to say to him. What could I have said?

I thought about this a thousand times as I walked back to Aunt Astrid's apartment. She is the only person I have left in the world. I would have to talk to her soon, tell her about Rafael Ruiz, my deceased biological grandfather, who for her, father's half-sister, would be some sort of relative. I couldn't figure out what. I would call her next week when she returned from her Caribbean vacation. While I was thinking that, a kind of anxiety overcame me; I felt that all my childhood memories, especially those of Mom who passed away when I was twelve years old, were hopelessly fading. Dad was always the one who remembered our lives, with the precision that characterized him; my memories were unreliable, they were light and imprecise at best.

I breathed in and out slowly to gather my wits. I had decided to have fun that night at the party, to escape a little from the intensity of those days. I was about to take another sip of the mezcal when Ricardo, Ana, and Natalia came to my side, as well as the newcomers, who happened to be two Mexican couples who had just started their doctoral studies; I knew them by sight. Ricardo introduced us and served drinks for everyone.

Just then the dance music started with a song that Ana and I liked, *El álbum* by Los Aterciopelados. As if we were all on the same page, we went as a group to the dance floor. At some point, Ana and I began to twirl with the song. The colored lights that bathed the Empire State Building changed, I noticed. First from purple to burgundy, then they turned blue.

THREE

A strong stomachache woke me up at dawn, and I had to go to the hospital's emergency room. The doctor on duty greeted me with a handshake and asked me what happened. It took me a few moments to speak; the doctor's last name, Vartatian, was the same as that of my academic advisor and chair of my dissertation committee. It occurred to me that they might be blood relatives; her piercing eyes and thick eyebrows reminded me of him.

I told her that I was not used to drinking spirits; I couldn't think of what else to say. The doctor said, "It could be that" and wrote something down in a notebook. She then asked me about my family's medical history. I informed her that Mom had died of thyroid cancer when I was twelve and my Aunt Astrid, Dad's sister, was in good health; I added that she was vegan, on account of nothing. Then, I explained to her, the best way I could, about Dad's early dementia –it's a complicated diagnosis– and his decision to quit working.

The doctor thanked me and watched me intently; then she looked at her notes.

"Before I let you go," she said, "I want you to do some additional blood work."

"What for?" I asked.

"They are normal procedures in a case like yours, to rule out other possible causes. The nurse will be here in a few minutes for a blood sample. She will give you an appointment at my office next week."

"I suspect that it might be something genetic," I told Ana when the doctor left.

"Where do you get that from?" Ana asked, wrinkling her forehead.

"I don't know. A hunch. Intuition. I don't know."

"I doubt that it's anything like your dad's," Ana countered. "You are too young for that. I'm sure the tests that the doctor ordered will clear that up."

"You're right," I said. "On the other hand, there is the issue of my biological grandfather, which makes matters more complicated, as a matter of fact."

"Your biological grandfather? What are you talking about?"

"It's a multi-chapter story," I said, and I told her about the photos I saw and what D'Artagnan had revealed to me.

"I don't understand the bit about the bargueño," Ana said, looking me in the eye. "Is it the same one your dad gave you, the one we have in the living room?"

I nodded.

"Pánfilo! You didn't tell me it had such a complex backstory".

"It's gotten complex recently. I didn't know that it was one of the antiques that had been stolen from us in Bogotá."

"How and when was that?"

"I would have been seven or eight years old. What I'm going to tell you is the version that my father told me."

"One day a distinguished-looking Spanish man came to my family's antique store. He wore an ascot scarf around his throat, a pretentious and unusual garment. Apparently, he had fine manners, though somewhat theatrical, and he spoke with a very strong Madrid accent. He said his name was Rosiñol del Valle and asked my father if he had colonial bargueños for sale; he explained that he was a collector of taracea antiques, recently relocated to Bogotá. He added that he worked at the Cultural Affairs Office of the Spanish Embassy and gave him his business card."

"Wow, cultural affairs," Ana interrupted. "The plot thickens," she added, and put an elbow on the table and a hand on her cheek.

"Dad said yes, he was one of the few antique dealers in the city who had that kind of furniture and asked him to follow him to the storage room. He would normally have shown him some photos from the catalog, but he sensed that he was a serious collector. The man examined one of the bargueños carefully for several minutes and asked if he had the certificate of authenticity. Dad said the documentation was in order and added that he also had for sale the illuminated bestiary from the 16th century, which the certificate of authenticity mentioned as the inspiration for its design. Rosiñol del Valle replied, of course, how appropriate, and declared that he would like to acquire them both if they agreed on a fair price. They went to Dad's office, and after half an hour agreed on fifty thousand dollars, which Rosiñol del Valle would pay with a cashier's check from his bank the next day, which by chance was also the bank where my father had his accounts. When the man left, Dad called the Cultural Affairs Office at the Spanish Embassy to make sure the man was who he said he was and was told that he had been recently appointed to his post and that he was a serious collector of Spanish Colonial Art. The next day the man came in the afternoon before closing, gave Dad the cashier's check and took the bargueño and the bestiary."

"But the check bounced."

"Yes, I have already told you."

"And what did they say at the bank?"

"That the check looked genuine, but it was the work of a very skilled forger. An artist," they said.

"An artist?"

That really upset Dad.

"And at the embassy?"

"There was no reply from the Cultural Affairs Office, so he called the embassy's main number and was told that no one with that name worked there. The telephone number on the business card was private, obviously part of the scam."

"Wow. What a character, Rosiñol del Valle!"

"Dad got depressed. As I told you before that was one of the reasons behind our move to New York. He had the bargueño insured, but the insurance company didn't pay the actual sale amount. I don't know how much in total; Dad doesn't like to talk about money."

"And how did your biological grandfather get it back?"

"I have no idea and I'm not sure I want to find out. Why didn't Dad tell me the truth? I thought I had a sense –a story– of my roots. I knew by heart the stories that Grandfather Gustavo told me about his life and that of his parents, my great-grandparents, and other members of that family, which now turns out not to be mine..."

FOUR

The appointment with Dr. Vartatian left me with more questions than answers. She first assured me that I didn't have any illnesses but then said that I was a *carrier* of a rare congenital disease and could pass it on to my children. She recommended it would be wise to do blood work on all members of my immediate family. She added that it was important to proceed as soon as possible. Then, she explained that my dad's early dementia could be one of the manifestations of that disease and said that she would like to go over his medical records; she wanted to see what kind of tests they had done. She was surprised when I told her that Dad was in Bogotá. She asked me why he had not stayed in New York and commented that she didn't know any experts in this type of rare disease in Colombia and that she would have to do an online search to get up to speed on that.

From Dr. Vartatian's office, on eighty-ninth and Madison, I walked home. It took me almost an hour and a half. The day was a bit cold and windy, but the sky was clear, and the sun was bright. I needed to calmly digest what the doctor had told me. I understood that as a carrier of this disease, I should carefully consider whether I wanted to have children, a question that I had never contemplated before and that inevitably led to the question of whether my future was with

Ana; she had once told me that if we took it to the next level and decided to get married, she would like to have at least two children.

As I walked, I turned the matter around, and imagined various scenarios, but did not come to any conclusion; I didn't need it back then either.

When I got home, I made a cup of herbal tea and called Tía Astrid. I told her to make herself comfortable, for I had news that would surprise her and perhaps also upset her.

"Did something happen to you, cariño?" she asked.

"Santo y salvo –holy and safe–" I replied, I knew that saying that would reassure her; according to Dad, as children, they used invented idioms that Mom and I learned. Santo y salvo meant, "no one noticed," "I have enough of something, money, for example," or "I'm full."

"I'm glad," she said, though her tone was of concern.

"I'm listening," she added.

Whenever I talked with Tía Astrid, I imagined her sitting in the living room of her cramped apartment chockfull of colonial antiques, on a steep street in the Chapinero district, in Bogotá, looking out over the sprawling city to the West, sipping a hot chocolate, her favorite drink, or a linden flower herbal tea like the one I was drinking.

Tía Astrid listened to my story without interrupting me, something unusual for her. Her silence made me think that what I had just told her was something she already suspected.

"Send me the photos," she said in a muted tone, as if she was losing her voice. "I have to see to believe."

"This very afternoon," I assured her.

"Who would have known that Grandma Francisca had..."

"Who would have believed it?" I would say, she added after a pause. "It's unbelievable. Really! I still can't believe it. Have you already seen the documents?"

"No," I replied. "Dad must have seen them, but I don't know, I don't think he made any copies." "Or maybe yes," I corrected myself, I remembered that I had some of Dad's documents somewhere.

"We have to find those documents," Tía Astrid urged. "I'll get right to it; the things that Gustavo brought from New York are in my storage room."

"And we have to look for the family, Rafael Ruiz's other family if he had one. Didn't D'Artagnan tell you something about it?"

"No, Tía, he didn't mention another family. He would have told me. Either way, I will ask him."

"Hmm," she murmured.

I didn't say anything else. I usually avoided mentioning D'Artagnan to Tía Astrid. She didn't get along with him; she said he was not her cup of tea. She is older than him, by eight or ten years I think, but she treats him, she treated him, as if he were my age, as if he were a friend of mine and not of my father's. Dad's theory about it was that Tía Astrid had a crush on him. They had something going on for a while. He told me that when she lived with us, she and D'Artagnan would go dancing at Latin clubs in Queens or Manhattan; they both liked tropical music, salsa, and merengue. He also told me that he teased them when they went to parties because they would only dance with each other and always in the same couple dancing style whether it was salsa, jazz, rock, or rhythm and blues.

"And what kind of blood tests does the doctor want?"

"I'll email that to you Tía," I replied.

"Now I remember something," she said, suddenly animated. "Dr. Carrizosa, who was always our client, and his family too, called me one day, two years ago more or less. It was not unusual for him to call me –the sweet old man– he did it from time to time, every two or three months. He was always very nice to me, and he also liked to talk about history and politics. Sometimes we would talk at length about something that he was writing about for the weekly magazine that his father founded and of which he was still part of the editorial committee. That day he asked me if he still had the technical file of the bargueño with the animal engravings that Rosiñol del Valle stole from your father. I told him no and speculated that Gustavo might have kept it. He thanked me and said that he was going to write to him. I asked him why he needed it and he told me that through his lawyer he had learned that there was a bargueño of uncertain origin but of similar characteristics–though not an antique, it was made twenty years ago– for sale at an auction house in London. He wanted to confirm whether it was a copy of the older stolen bargueño. I wished him good luck and forgot all about it. But now it occurs to me that your biological grandfather might be the taracea master who made the copy, the one at the auction house in London. The stolen bargueño–your bargueño–is very unique and it would be very difficult to make a copy of it unless you have access to it. Since your biological grandfather did restorations for your grandfather Gustavo, he may be the one who made it."

"How very astute of you," I said.

"It's a possibility. Perhaps the missing documents can give us a clue."

"I'll do my part," I said.

"I just remembered another conversation with the sweet old man Carrizosa," Tía Astrid said, once again suddenly animated. "This was a few months after the other conversation I just told you about, but I didn't connect the dots then, I don't know why. That day I had just returned from teaching an English class at the Institute. The phone was ringing when I opened the door, the sweet old man always called me on the landline, he didn't like cell phones, he said that he didn't understand why people had to talk on the phone from anywhere. He told me that a friend of his who is a collector of colonial art learned that there was a bargueño for sale in Madrid that had the same characteristics down to the measurements as one of the bargueños at Casa de Nariño, the presidential palace in Bogotá. He said he saw pictures of it and found the likeness remarkable. He noted that the engravings were very well done, the work of a true artist. The only difference was that the bargueño in Madrid was new, and the one in the presidential palace is attributed to an XVI-century artisan from Bogotá. He asked me whether I knew of any artisans who might be able to do such work. I told him, no, that to my knowledge there wasn't anyone in Colombia who could pull that off."

"Do you think my biological grandfather also made that one?"

"I don't think so," Tía Astrid replied. "It's possible but not likely. I looked at the pictures of the bargueños on the presidential palace's website. You can't see a lot of detail; they were taken from afar. And the pictures only show it from a three-quarter view, which doesn't give you enough information to draw a plan, much less to figure out what is on the top, the bottom, and the back."

"Unless he had the plans or had access to it," I ventured.

"Two years ago, your biological grandfather was already an old man," Tía Astrid pointed out. "At least eighty, your dad was already sixty-two. I don't think so."

FIVE

Ana was going to be away from home all day, she always spent Saturdays with her aunt and her cousins who lived on the Upper West Side. She asked me to go with her; she said it was time for me to meet that part of her family, but I told her I wasn't in the mood, I kept thinking about that new grandfather that I never met. She shrugged and warned that one of these days I was going to run out of excuses.

The truth is that the prospect of meeting Ana's family intimidated me. From what she'd told me, we had nothing in common. They were wealthy people, principals of an important trading company in Colombia on the mother's side and, on the father's side, cattle ranchers and landowners. Aunt Margarita, Ana's mother's sister, was a painter and poet, and her husband was a renowned oncologist at Sloan Kettering Center in Manhattan, a medical center specializing in cancer treatment. Ana's two cousins were the same age as us. The youngest was a graduate of NYU's Creative Writing Program and worked for a television production company in Hudson Yards and the oldest had just finished a PhD in Art History at Columbia and was working at a well-known auction house in Rockefeller Center. Ana got along well with them, although they inhabited different social worlds. Ana used to say that she was halfway between my world of middle-class immigrants in Queens, which depending on the neighborhood might as well be somewhere in the developing world, and her wealthy relatives in the exclusive Upper West Side, a world I was only acquainted with through literature and film. The other big difference, apart from the astronomical gap in financial well-being, at least in my case, is, as Ana has told me many times, that they are people who are worldly and sophisticated. They've traveled east and west, south and north, and speak and read and write in three languages, including French, and they all attended high school in Geneva, a family tradition, it seems. In contrast, I am hardly bilingual, and, apart from Bogotá and London where I spent an academic semester abroad, I don't know any other places. D'Artagnan told me that Ana and I should go to Paris this summer, we could stay in his apartment –he still owned it–, his ex-wife would be on vacation in Greece and his daughter was going to spend the summer with him in New York. However, it was a luxury that I couldn't afford; the money from my student loans were barely enough to cover my expenses.

After I had my breakfast, I dumped the box containing some of Dad's things on the dining room table. It was mostly business correspondence from the antique store, a couple of novels, a few DVDs of Colombian rock bands, and the keys to our apartment in Astoria. I looked at the documents front and back to make sure there was nothing written on them, Dad sometimes made notes about important things on whatever was at hand at the moment, but I found nothing of importance. One of the novels was by Antonio Tabucchi, an Italian writer, and the other by George Eliot, his favorite writer, in English, and mine too; I browsed them a couple of times and found nothing out of the ordinary.

It occurred to me that the only place I could find a clue would be Dad's laptop that he gave me before he left. I took it out of the desk drawer where I had it. I used his password, it was the date of his and Mom's wedding, 23091981. I rummaged through the folders, but there was nothing, not a single document. I looked at his email, I knew the password, but I didn't find anything out of the ordinary; Dad only used email for business.

Frustrated with my search, I threw myself over the sofa with Tabucchi's novel, *Indian Nocturne* in hand. I browsed over it again – it was a book I liked, too – and looked for one of the paragraphs that Dad had underlined. It was a scene where Xavier, the protagonist, talks to the director of the Theosophical Society in Madras in India, a city that is now called Chennai. The theosophist tells him something that is part of a poem by Fernando Pessoa:

'Blind science tills vain clods, mad faith lives the dream of its cult, a new God is only a word. Do not believe or search, everything is hidden.'

I woke up suddenly, I didn't realize that I had fallen asleep. Tabucchi's novel was lying on the floor.

After a quick instant noodle soup for lunch, I decided to take a walk around Greenwich Village or SoHo; I would decide on the go. Walking through the city streets helped me think. I needed to untangle the knots in my head, I was feeling overwhelmed with everything that was happening to me.

As I walked out to the Union Square Subway station, I felt slightly flushed. I was wearing my signature trench coat that Ana had given me for Christmas, a very formal and elegant garment for my taste; it was not something I would have chosen. I felt like I was wearing a 1970s detective or spy costume.

Crossing Washington Square, I remembered that in the first year of my Ph.D. coursework, before I hooked up with Ana, I would meet Dad near the marble arch on Friday afternoons around seven to go out to dinner. I always found him feeding the pigeons, something that completely absorbed his attention. It's manna from heaven for them, he would say, another made-up idiom, which meant apart from the sacred bread of the Jewish exile, the fortuitous solution of a problem, money earned, or the most common at home, the food was delicious.

For no other reason than to immerse myself in those not-too-distant memories, I sat down on one of the benches and stretched my arms and legs. The sky was full of round, billowing white clouds; altogether they looked like a flock of sheep.

Every single time we met there, Dad and I would go to *Natsuko*, a Japanese restaurant off Christopher Street, on the ground floor of a handsome brick building that might once have been a tenement. The owner or manager, Noriko-san was a Japanese woman about Dad's age with whom he was very kind, even affectionate. He always talked to her, asked her about this and that, and paid her a compliment that often made her blush. One day, I asked him how long he had known her, and he told me that for many years he and Mom had often gone to dinner there when I was a child, at the time when Tía Astrid lived with us and helped us with housework. Back then, Mom worked full time at the Jefferson Market Public Library, in a Victorian Gothic building on Sixth Avenue and Tenth Street, ten minutes on foot from the marble arch. On that occasion, he also told me that he and Mom had always wanted to live in the Village, but unfortunately, the rents in that area were always out of reach. I couldn't help but think about our apartment in Astoria, in Queens. I lived all my life there until Dad went back to Colombia, and I moved with Ana to Tudor City, in Manhattan. It was in one of those residential complexes so common in the city of red brick apartment buildings. It had three narrow bedrooms with plenty of natural light, a 1970s kitchen with Formica counters, and an extended living and dining room with large windows that opened onto one of the complex's playgrounds. I didn't like that it was near an elevated subway station; in the months when we had the windows open, you could hear the constant rattling of the trains and the buzzing sound before the closing of the doors of the cars. Ironically, now that I live on a quieter street, I miss those railway noises, especially in the early mornings.

    After a few minutes of reminiscing, I decided that I would go by the Japanese restaurant and take some photos of its ornate wooden facade. For some time, I had been taking photographs of places in the city that caught my attention; time would tell if it was worthwhile. Then, I would go to my favorite bookstore on Carmine Street. Hopefully, I would meet the owner with whom I used to sometimes talk about authors we liked. He also gave me a good discount.

When I got to my feet, I was surprised: I saw Vartatian rush across the path a few feet away from me; I assumed he was heading to the library. It seemed peculiar to me that he was carrying a bulky backpack, perhaps full of books that he had to return. I wanted to call out to him, but I held back. I didn't have anything to say to him, and besides, he looked rushed. I saw him walk away and turn right onto Fourth Street. He wasn't going to the library. It occurred to me that he was also going to the bookstore on Carmine; after all, they bought and sold used books, which was what Vartatian could be carrying in his bulky backpack. Without thinking twice and with no plan in case he saw me, I followed him at a good distance. I got along well with Vartatian, but our relationship was purely professional. We were not friends, although since he became my advisor, I'd had the feeling that he wanted us to be friends, or at least have more personal contact.

Vartatian continued south on MacDougal, confirming my suspicion of our common destination. But instead of turning right on First Street, he walked straight ahead. I thought, 'Thank goodness we're not going to the same place,' but right away, I told myself that I had to know where he was going, as long as he wasn't going very far. I followed him, keeping a safe distance. I promised myself that if he crossed Houston, several streets down, I would give up, though

I wasn't sure whether I would be able to keep that promise. I was often obsessed with my tasks and projects; I couldn't leave anything half-done. As I contemplated this, I saw Vartatian enter a store that turned out to be Goldfinch Antiques. I crossed the street and hid in the shade of a fashion store awning, my eyes fixed on the door of the antique store.

After eight or ten minutes, which seemed like an eternity, I saw Vartatian come out, but he was no longer carrying the backpack. After hesitating for an instant, he continued to walk south, probably towards the MacDougal Street subway station, Vartatian lived in Midtown in Hell's Kitchen, and he could take any northbound train. I waited a few moments until he was out of sight and crossed the street. I wanted to take a look at the antique store, but when I reached the door, a bald, middle-aged man, put up the 'Sorry We're Closed' sign and turned around. I doubt he even saw me.

On the way to the Carmine Street bookstore, I remembered that one time when we were going to Natsuko with Dad, he told me about a disagreement he had many years ago with an antique dealer in the Village about the value of Spanish colonial antiques. I was worried about something related to my financial aid at school and didn't pay much attention to it. What I remember clearly is that that night he warned me, for the umpteenth time, never to get into the antique business. It's full of bandits, he added.

SIX

It was pouring rain when I got home. I sat on the sofa in the living room to contemplate the spectacle. Our tiny studio apartment had a panoramic view of the East River, Roosevelt Island, and the cantilever Queensboro Bridge on Fifty-ninth, which links Manhattan to my old neighborhood in Queens.

The rain fell monotonously in gusts that billowed from side to side, whipping from time to time against the windowpanes. The spectacle engrossed me and unleashed memories of my last two years of high school when I would go for a walk along the other side of the river, in Astoria, almost every day. There were many times that I was caught in a downpour, but I never ran for cover, under a building's awning, for example. On the contrary, I submitted, I surrendered myself to the water, and I let myself be soaked to the skin. I have always loved the feeling of the rain dripping down my body. Apart from that, it stirred my imagination, it made me see the thread of a story or the shadow of a poem that I had to write.

The downpour suddenly worsened, as did the clattering against the windows, which became a roar at intervals. The other side of the river faded slowly behind the rain clouds until it disappeared. My eyes fixed on the curtain of clouds;

I remembered a rainy afternoon at Grandfather Gustavo's house in Bogotá. I was seven or maybe eight years old. It was a Sunday; my grandfather always invited us to lunch that day. My world at that time was all in Spanish, I knew only a few phrases in English, learned in school. That afternoon, I was very surprised to hear Dad speak on the phone in that language. I had the strange feeling that he was someone else, not just from the sound of the words but from his entire attitude; he made gestures with his hands and with his face that I'd never seen him do. I asked Mom and she told me that he had learned English in New York through an exchange program arranged by his High School. Her response surprised me, and from that day on I became interested in everything to do with New York: magazine articles, television shows, and above all, movies.

I was going to the kitchen to make a cup of herbal tea when Ana opened the door.

"I'm soaked," she said and went into the bathroom.

"Aunt Margarita invited us to lunch next Saturday," she announced.

"We'll see," I replied.

Ana repeated my words twice in a mocking tone and then added something I couldn't understand, perhaps an onomatopoeia; she often did that when she was in a good mood.

Instead of making herbal tea, I poured two glasses of wine and put them on the coffee table.

She came out of the bathroom wearing the floral print Kimono robe I gave her for Christmas, and on her head a towel rolled up like a turban. She sat on her knees facing me, her feet bare.

You always say, *'we'll see'*, pirata, when you want to say, *'I'll think about it'*.

"Well, let's say yes," I conceded, and nodded. Sooner or later, we will have to.

I surprised myself that I had said that, and also that I didn't hesitate.

"You won't regret it, I promise you," Ana said and kissed me on the cheek.

"I saw Vartatian at an antique store in the Village," I said.

"What was he up to?"

"That's the $64,000 question," I said and started to tell Ana how I had followed him, but for some reason, my words got tangled up and I ended up saying it in English.

Ana looked at me in surprise. "First time I heard you code-switching."

"You see, I forget my Spanish when I need it most."

"Like it or not, you are more gringo than Colombian."

"Dad always said that if I code-switched without realizing it, or if I made a mistake with a word. He meant it as a reproach, but it didn't work on me, or at least not to the extent Dad wanted. It was a bit ironic that he said that because I could've turned the tables around and said *that* of him, and with good reason."

"I understand," Ana said and took a sip of wine.

"Sorry, I'm always going back to the same thing."

"Nothing is ever the same," she said.

We both looked towards the East River; the downpour had turned into a monotonous drizzle.

"Have you decided how to formulate your project?" Ana asked.

"No, not really," I replied. "However, I'm still considering interviewing three immigrant families from diverse backgrounds. I plan to include a section on lived experiences and then expand on my review of the literature on literary anthropology."

"I'm curious about what you meant by formulating," I commented. It's also used in medicine, right?

"Yes, doctors, I mean medical doctors, can formulate, that is, write prescriptions."

"And the doctors of philosophy?"

"They formulate *Pharmakon*."

"You're always so Greek".

"What's holding you back, Francisco? You have to submit your research proposal in two weeks."

"If I knew, we wouldn't be having this conversation."

"I'm listening. Perhaps I can help you."

"I've already told you, Ana. It's a crisis of faith, in the project, and in myself."

"It may be that you expect too much of yourself."

"That happens to all of us. Sorry, I am not expressing myself well..."

"I don't think so. I get it. Really."

"I know, thanks. Perhaps I made it complicated."

"You're not sure whether you are going to write your ethnography as an essay or as a novel?"

"That, to begin with," I said.

"You wanted to be a writer since you were little, right?"

"That was what Dad wanted; he wanted me to become a writer. Since he noticed that I liked literature, he started buying complete series of this and that. He was the one who insisted that I take elective classes in creative writing in high school."

"And you didn't want to?"

"I've told you that I did, but it wasn't a priority for me. Besides, I was in an identity crisis, almost in the same way that I am now; I didn't have much confidence in myself. And, to top it off, I convinced myself that I had a disadvantage because I was an immigrant, a child of immigrants, always navigating two worlds."

"You never saw that as an advantage?"

"In my old age," I said. "Ironically, it was the first graduate courses in ethnographic writing that made me see things differently."

"It's never too late, dear pirata," Ana pointed out and looked towards the East River. A cargo barge sailed silently towards the open sea, a red lightbulb on the bow. The night was falling.

SEVEN

On the evening of Ana's birthday, we decided to go with Natalia and Ricardo to a Vietnamese restaurant in Greenwich Village. We often went there though always as a group. Ana and I didn't know much about Asian cuisines and were happy to let our friends guide us. Apart from being gastronomic adventurers, they traveled through several of those countries and knew their cultures and customs. That night we were also celebrating being selected to teach a class on topics related to my research in the undergraduate division of the university next semester.

When we left the university, it was snowing copiously. There was already a bright blanket of snow on the street that contrasted with the gray cloak of clouds up in the sky. Natalia said that she 'loved snow, it brought her good luck', and Ricardo commented, 'we have plenty of luck what we need is cash'. I wanted to add to the banter, but something held me back and instead I pointed out that there was a lull in traffic and that we should cross Fifth Avenue. We walked briskly and huddled under our coats the best way we could. The restaurant was on the corner of Grove and Bleecker, a few blocks south of Natsuko where we went with Dad, and roughly the same distance east of D'Artagnan's bar, although to go to these three places from the university I took different routes; The Village is like that, nothing can be reached following a straight line.

Snowfall always makes me sad. It reminds me of Mom, who passed on the night of a snowstorm, back in '92. When it snows, I can't help but remember the moment when Dad gave me the bad news. I was in the waiting room at Lenox Hill Hospital, watching the snow fall on the street ten or twelve floors below. By the reflection of the window, I saw that he was coming towards me and from the look on his face, I understood what had happened.

For some reason I don't understand, my memory has gradually transformed itself. For some time now, I see myself in that fateful moment divided into two: the one who sees Dad and his somber expression on the window, and the other, who is actually me, who watches that scene from across the street, and understands that his life has changed forever. In this new split-in-two memory, I hear something, a hollow noise behind me, like that of a branch that falls on the white blanket of snow and breaks the silence of my desolation. I don't know why my memory has become like this; sometimes I think it is a riddle that I have to solve. Something that is submerged in my unconscious and comes up to the surface when it snows in the city. I have not shared this memory with anyone, not even with Dad, who is now the only person who knows me well, or knew me well; we haven't gotten there with Ana, but we are on the right track.

We had to wait a while at the narrow entrance of the restaurant; there were no free tables. That evening, they had a large group of Asian tourists. To pass the time, Ricardo and

Natalia asked me how I was and whether I had done the tests the doctors recommended. I told them I was waiting for the results, which would take at least two weeks. I didn't get into specifics; I wanted to avoid talking about Dr. Vartatian's suspicions, much less about my biological grandfather. At some point I would tell them, but some other time.

As was our custom whenever we met for dinner, we began to talk about our department. In the last few weeks, we'd received two pieces of bad news that were starting to cast a shadow on the reputation of our graduate program and somehow on our future in academia. The first and perhaps the most alarming was that two of our senior professors had announced that they had accepted job offers elsewhere. The second was that the university's administration was considering restructuring, or perhaps closing one or more departments, though they had not said which. The rumors were vague; it could've been mere speculation by some nervous administrator.

"Did you hear the gossip about Vartanian?" Natalia asked out of the blue.

Ana and I looked at each other and shook our heads. Ricardo, who surely already knew what it was about, gave us one of his sarcastic smiles.

I felt a knot in my stomach. It occurred to me that perhaps Vartanian was also thinking of leaving, and I was the last one to know about it. If he left, I would have to find a new dissertation chair, and it wasn't possible to have an external one.

"He is in love with a sociology student," Ana stated, repeating a rumor she had heard from some classmates who followed some of our professors' private lives like paparazzi, constantly on the lookout for sensational news.

"That's not it," Natalia teased like a game show hostess. "But if that were true, Marta would crucify him."

"At the very least," Ana put in, "she was also a student of Marta Salazar, Vartanian's Colombian wife, who was the true star of the department."

"I'll give you a hint," Natalia went on in her game show tone of voice. "It has to do with one of his projects."

"The Colombian Truth Commission," Ana ventured, "she was Vartanian's Teaching Assistant and spent a lot of time in his office."

"You hit the nail on the head, darling," Natalia replied and added that it was 'top secret'. She made us promise not to tell anyone, and once we did, she told us that Vartanian had to rewrite the Introduction and the Conclusion of his manuscript because of revelations made by a high-ranking Army officer regarding the so-called *false positives,* innocent civilians killed, and presented to the authorities as guerrilla fighters. She said that she learned that from a former classmate who was a copyeditor, who by cosmic coincidence worked part-time at the university press that was going to publish Vartanian's latest book and was in charge of fact-checking and copyediting.

Ricardo commented that he wasn't surprised. He always declared that Vartanian wanted everything to fit into his theoretical framework, the world upside down. Natalia agreed with him and speculated that it was perhaps the reason he had been so sullen of late and didn't want to see anyone in his office.

I was already aware of the matter, Vartanian had told me, also in confidence, so I refrained from speaking. Besides, I didn't want to ruin my friends' pleasure of gossiping about Vartanian's bad news, or his flaws and weaknesses. Unlike his wife, he wasn't popular with his students. Most of us admired him, but for some reason, perhaps his disheveled nature and perennial bad temper –the strongest contrast to his popular wife– didn't arouse in us any affection or loyalty.

Although I followed the conversation, there was something else that bothered me about Vartanian: his insistence that I consult with a colleague of his at Fordham, who turned out to be a visiting professor of Colombian origin. I went to see him last Thursday, after my classes. His name was Tomás Rodrigues, and he was a full professor at a Japanese Jesuit university in Tokyo who specialized in sixteenth-century Japan, though in recent years had worked on topics related to Latin American immigrant communities in Japan, which I assumed was the reason why Vartanian wanted me to see him. When I told him about my dissertation project, he commented that he found it fascinating since he was interested in everything related to diasporas, and he would gladly read whatever I wanted to share. I wanted to ask Rodrigues what relationship he had with Vartanian, but I thought better of it. I figured I wouldn't lose anything in hearing or reading his comments, whatever they were; after all, what counted was the opinion of the members of my Dissertation Committee.

A sudden burst of laughter from Ana and our friends brought me out of my thoughts.

"Did you hear what Natalia just told us?" Ana asked, a grimace on her face.

"I was distracted for a moment," I said. "What is it?"

"She's pregnant. They're going to have a child!"

"Really?"

"We're already nine weeks," Ricardo said and smiled from ear to ear.

"Congratulations," I said, as best I could, my throat was suddenly dry. Truly, I added a little louder and placed my hands over those of Natalia and Ricardo who were sitting across from me, a gesture that was not mine but Dad's, he always did that when we ate at home when Mom was alive; it was a gesture of affection, although a stranger might think it a prelude to a prayer, a blessing of the table.

Natalia looked me in the eye, perhaps surprised by my gesture, and said that if it were a boy they would name him Francisco, after her favorite Spanish poet, Francisco de Quevedo. Ricardo said, a smirk on his face, "you see, my friend, I'm not allowed to name my own son. If it were up to me, I would name him *Calibán*, to keep on with the literary vibe. But if it's a girl, it is up to me," he said again a smirk on his face, "so I will name her Hellena with a double l, or Ariadna, names from antiquity that contain mysterious and unforgettable stories."

"We'll see, we'll see," Natalia said and took her hand away from under mine. Ricardo did the same and took a sip of the beer they had just served him. Ana took the initiative and proposed a toast to our friendship and the future of that new life on the way.

At that moment, I saw a flurry of snow fall from the building across the street, perhaps from a ledge from a higher floor. From where I was sitting, I could only see a small portion of the brick masonry façade, bathed in the yellow of the street lamps.

The sight brought a lump to my throat, and suddenly, I felt the need to step outside and run away from it all.

EIGHT

When we got back home, Ana asked me what was wrong with me. She said that I was distracted and uneasy during dinner and that my congratulations to Natalia and Ricardo had seemed flat and insincere. I told her I was not in the mood to talk about it; I would do it soon when I had time to think a little. But as it always happens to me with Ana, my clumsy attempts to evade a conversation topic became the object of scrutiny and analysis. "What is it that you have to think about?" she asked. "Whatever it is, you can tell me. The two of us can figure things out. I'm sure it will help you." I tried to get out of it by saying that I wasn't feeling well, but Ana stood her ground and suggested not feeling well was just an excuse, and that sooner or later I would have to face reality. As if this were not enough, she added that perhaps I should "return to therapy," something that irritated me deeply. Once again, I felt the need to run away from it all like I'd felt at the restaurant, but I held back and remained silent.

"Fantastic," Ana said. "That's the smart way to handle the situation." She folded her arms, her prelude to battle.

To prevent the situation from getting out of hand, I opened my laptop and pretended to be busy with a last-minute task. Ana looked at me for a moment, a frown on her brow, and said she was going to go to bed. She turned off all the lights just to bother me.

Our fights were always like that. They started with a reproach for something of no consequence, followed by an attempt to analyze my behavior, to examine it with a sort of psychological microscope, and if that failed, it would escalate to open warfare in which Ana's favorite weapons were retaliatory accusations for this and that, rarely ever related to the initial issue; and mine were complaints that what she was saying was irrelevant, cruel, or unnecessary. I often forgot that as a last resort, I begged her not to treat me like a child, which Ana used to deliver the final blow and say: 'you see, you yourself know what's wrong with you': 'you're still a spoiled child, you need to grow up and mature.' So far, however, all those unpleasant moments had been followed by other pleasant moments of reconciliation, often in bed. Ana could not bear the icy silence that followed our disagreements or quarrels, and almost always it was she who capitulated, as long as I agreed, of course. She didn't allow me to be angry any longer than she was.

I thought about it for a moment and told myself I was an idiot for letting myself be carried away by my bad temper. I could very well have told her what had happened to me, or rather what happens to me on snowy days in this city. This was our first winter living together. The year and a half we spent as lovers didn't quite tally, considering we each had our place, a private haven for emotional outbursts. However, I kept it to myself. I hesitated to confide in her because I felt ashamed of admitting that I hadn't fully overcome my mother's passing. What was probably coming upon me was a kind of perfect storm, where the initial loss of my mother loomed to merge with the impending loss of my father, who might have already forgotten that my mother and I ever existed...

I told myself that, perhaps, Ana was right, and I should go back to therapy. However, no sooner had the thought crossed my mind—of seeing myself on the couch, so to speak—than something within me insisted it wouldn't work. What was happening to me felt fluid and temporary, likely to dissipate or vanish completely with the arrival of spring and my eventual freedom from classes and exams at the university.

While lost in contemplation, my eyes gradually adjusted to the darkness, allowing me to discern the contours of our furniture. Street lamps below cast just enough light. Like many, I have a fear of complete darkness, yet I find solace in dimmed lights. Seated at one end of the dining room table, facing away from the kitchen, I could see the shelves of our bookcases, which Ana constantly organizes with a librarian's zeal. She can't bear to see a book out of place. She's like this with everything: clothes, CDs and DVDs, even tools and cutlery. In this aspect, we differ. It's not that I dislike organization or that I'm disorganized, but I don't mind if a novel or a book of poetry finds itself in the anthropology section or if an Italian film coexists with documentaries.

There was a time I clashed with Ana. While I was out shopping, she took it upon herself to organize some of my father's things from a cardboard box mistakenly placed on the bottom shelf of Ana's side of the bookcase. The box held various documents, letters, photographs, and newspaper clippings that my father had not taken to Colombia. Upon discovering her rummaging through the box, I couldn't control myself and, perhaps not in the best way, told her to leave it there. I explained it contained my father's personal effects, which I intended to send to him—a lie, I must admit, and guilt weighed on me for not doing it sooner. At that point, Dad was already in a nursing home, his memory fading each day. Ana looked puzzled and told me that she only intended to sort out the contents of the box and that I shouldn't be such an ungrateful jerk. Ana's attitude and her comments made the situation worse, and for the first time since we started dating, I raised my voice. I couldn't help it. I told her that I didn't need her to do me any favors by organizing my stuff, as I knew exactly where everything was.

On the other hand, those differences had not been an obstacle in our relationship. Ana and I got along great. We always managed to agree on everything, even on academic and political issues. Not to mention, our tastes in film and literature coincided. The major difference, apart from the sense of order or perhaps one of its variants, was the way of handling our personal problems. Ana had blind faith in psychological interventions, especially in Lacanian therapy —a topic she liked to discuss from a theoretical standpoint. It didn't interest me in the least; it seemed unnecessarily complex and indulgent. Although as Ana pointed out, I didn't know enough about it to make an intelligent comment. Be that as it may, for Ana any crisis, no matter how small or large, warranted a good set of therapy sessions, especially if they had clear objectives.

Appeased and relaxed in the semi-darkness, I realized that what had most irritated me was Ana's suggestion to *return* to therapy. It seemed not only arrogant but also a malicious way of linking my past to the present. I did go to therapy for a while, five or six months, if I remember correctly. It was in the months that followed Mom's death. However, that was a long time ago when I was not who I am now. Like a fool, I told Ana the whole story a few months ago, and ever since, she brought it up whenever the opportunity presented itself. I closed my eyes and tried to remember what therapy had been like, and without much effort, the memories came to me —clear and sharp.

Dr. Amos, the psychoanalyst, was a middle-aged woman, tall and thin, with curly dark hair and a pleasant face that reminded me of a distant cousin who was much older than me. She always smiled at the beginning and end of our sessions, and the rest of the time, she looked at me intently, turning her head slightly to her right to listen to what I was saying, as if she had some sort of hearing problem. We usually talked about everyday, banal stuff: how I was doing at school, if I got along well with my friends, if I slept well, if I was reading a book that I liked. I elaborated on the answers and took it seriously. If the question did not merit a long answer, I would make something up, or rather, I would tell her things that friends or classmates had told me as if they had happened to me. Nothing extraordinary or otherworldly, just stuff that my father and I didn't do, like going to baseball or basketball games, sports that he hated and I liked. I watched them on TV when I was bored or when I couldn't think of anything else to do.

The doctor took notes in a leather-bound notebook of what I said, I suppose. Although sometimes, from the way she moved her hands and looked at me, I thought that she was drawing a portrait of the person she saw—which couldn't be me because that me only revealed itself on sleepless nights when everything was spinning in my head and my fears and certainties spoke out loud. The sessions ended abruptly in the winter of that year. My father never told me why; I assumed it was a matter of money. In the last session, the doctor told me that we had made quite a bit of progress, which I found strange and funny at the same time. I didn't understand what she meant by progress. Was it progress talking about the minutiae of my life? Or the fact that I no longer cried suddenly the way I did during the first months of therapy? Either way, our relationship ended, and I missed her for a while. Talking to her was engaging; I had a certain fascination with weaving made-up stories for her. After a few months, my memory of her faded despite the closeness—not to mention intimacy—that we had during our sessions.

I wondered if returning to therapy with the same analyst after almost twenty years would be wise. Immediately, an internal voice suggested that it would make sense. After all, Dr. Amos would have the notes and drawings from that time in her files, so we could pick up where we had left off.

After a few minutes, I felt calmer and decided to go to bed. I assumed Ana would already be asleep. She only had to lay her head on the pillow to fall into a deep sleep. I lay down and closed my eyes, intending to evoke my mother's image, but what came to mind was my father's, back in those faraway days when our wound was still fresh. He also went to see Dr. Amos but at different times than mine. What each of us discussed with her, we never brought up.

That marked the era of our long walks in Manhattan, spiced up by my father's comments and facts about movies shot in the city. He often spoke of becoming a New Yorker in Bogotá's cinemas in the 1970s and 1980s, watching films by directors like Sydney Lumet, Martin Scorsese, and Woody Allen, where New York was more than a backdrop—it was part of the cast. The one he mentioned the most was Woody Allen's Annie Hall, which he insisted on calling *Dos extraños amantes*, the Spanish language title used in Colombia in the late 1970s when my parents were dating and started to make the plans that would change their lives.

During our walks, my father would say things like: 'Look, Annie Hall lived there on 68th and Madison,' or: 'On this street Annie and Alvy walked hand in hand,' or 'Over there on 65th and Second was the cinema where they saw a Bergman film,' or 'In this corner on 63rd near Lincoln Center, they said goodbye the last time they saw each other when the two were already dating other people.'

Amidst those memories, I recalled a sleepless night many years ago, months after my mother's death, when I found Dad in the living room watching Annie Hall, the volume turned down. I didn't say anything or make any noise because it was one of his favorite scenes, where Diane Keaton sang,

Seems Like Old Times. I didn't want to interrupt his enjoyment. At home, we often listened to that song; we had the Thelma Carpenter and Ella Fitzgerald versions. Mom hummed it when she was in a good mood, usually when she was making dinner. Until then, I had not paid much attention to the lyrics, I was indifferent to that type of jazz from the 1940s at the time. However, that night when I listened to it, I realized that in some ways it was the musical theme of their relationship–the song accompanied their falling in love, which perhaps Dad was listening to, to summon the ghost of their happiness.

In the distance, I heard the first lines that Keaton sang with a smile between enigmatic and seductive:
'Seems like old times, having you to walk with
Seems like old times, having you to talk with.'

NINE

To my great amazement, the meeting with Vartatian about my research proposal went well. He appreciated the way I formulated the project and agreed with the methodology. His advice made sense, though it was somewhat surprising given his reputation for disciplinary orthodoxy. The main change he suggested was that I incorporate perspectives from other disciplines. He recommended a recent publication from a department of Comparative Literature and Anthropology at a university in Scotland, emphasizing the synergy between the two. As he told me this, the somewhat absurd idea occurred to me that he also wrote fiction, or he wanted to. I knew that Marta Salazar, his wife, also an anthropologist, had published several poems in literary and peer-reviewed magazines and journals.

The only dissonant note from the meeting was his suggestion to add his friend and colleague, Tomás Rodrigues, at Fordham, to my dissertation committee. He mentioned that Rodrigues had published a novel considered a good example of auto-ethnography and was compiling an anthology of short stories written by undocumented immigrants in Japan. I said that it was fine with me, I imagined it was a way to help his friend and colleague and didn't give it any more thought. At the end of the meeting, he told me that he was confident that I would do a good job and gave me a wide smile. He even shook my hand, something very unusual for him.

When I came out to the street, I sent text messages to Ana and Ricardo saying that everything had gone well. They were in class at the time. They had both read the draft of the proposal and had given me comments to improve it. I was frankly euphoric. Vartatian's support was all I needed to get into the next phase, my defense of the proposal before a committee. If that went well, and of that, I was almost certain, I would be ready to start fieldwork.

At the Union Square Subway station, I decided that instead of going straight home, I would go to the Metropolitan Museum first. It was one of my favorite places in the city. I hadn't been there for several months and figured it was the perfect reward for my success with Vartatian. Ana would not get home until six or six thirty, so I could take my time; it was still early afternoon, it was not even two o'clock.

On the subway, I thought of the times when Dad would take me to that imposing museum when I was little on Saturdays or Sundays. Mom would stay at home resting; years later, I found out that since we arrived in New York, she had been under continual treatment for thyroid cancer. We usually would spend an hour or two in the museum galleries, an eternity for me at first; with time I got used to it. More than looking at works of art, Dad contemplated them. He would fix his gaze on a piece from a distance, with a calm demeanor, but with a slight trace of concern on his face, as if he feared that something would suddenly happen within it. Once, I asked him what he was looking for in David's *Death of Socrates*, perhaps a precocious question for my age. In response, he vividly described the scene. I don't remember exactly what I said to him, I guess, "Thank you, Dad," as a child I was taught to be polite and formal. Occasionally, I tried to imitate his contemplation, but soon realized I didn't comprehend his intention or method. If a work failed to captivate me or if boredom set in, I'd declare my intention to move on. Dad would nod, release my hand, and instruct me not to wander. One day, my attention was drawn to a painting in the next gallery. An oil painting by Goya, the portrait of Manuel Osorio Manrique de Zúñiga—a boy, younger than me, gazing into the distance, oblivious to the danger posed by a magpie he holds with a cord on the floor, three cats poised to pounce. I guess the scene captivated me. Perhaps I identified with the boy's distant and withdrawn gaze, his somewhat mechanical attitude, like a doll that, over time, I have linked with an image that I have of myself in those early, and particularly difficult for me, years in New York. After a year in a transitional program at school, I lagged in almost every subject. My English proficiency was subpar; I could read and write, though poorly. I understood spoken English to a great extent but struggled to express myself verbally; my words would become tangled. For some reason, I couldn't *soltar la lengua*, loosen my tongue, as Mom would say—an expression that always sounded comical to me. At home, where we exclusively spoke Spanish, there was little to aid my improvement. We didn't watch television in English at that time. Gradually, I improved, but other obstacles lay ahead.

When the group of tourists moved to another room, Dad was no longer in front of the work he had contemplated a few minutes before. Later, he told me that for some reason he assumed that I had followed the group of tourists –apparently, I had done something like that before–so he went looking for them. For my part, I thought that Dad had forgotten about me, though quickly realized that it was absurd. It occurred to me that he had gone to the bathroom, and I went looking for him in the one closest to where I was; I knew where they were located. I called his name, but no one answered. When I turned to leave, I saw my face in the mirror. I had to stop and look again as if to make sure that it was indeed me; apart from the frown on my brow, I noticed on my face an expression of anguish that I had never seen before. I wandered about through the neighboring galleries looking for Dad. A guard asked me if I was lost, and I gave him an account of my situation, fluently and accurately, for the first time in English. I couldn't believe it! The man nodded and repeated the information I gave him through the public address system. Dad arrived in a few minutes looking a bit distressed. When he saw me, he shook his head, then he smiled and laughed. That afternoon we told Mom the story. At first, she gave us an odd look, and then, without saying a word, she gave us both a hug.

With that memory in mind, I got off at Seventy-Seventh and Lexington. I wanted to delay my arrival at the museum to once again concentrate on the moment when I spoke with the museum guard. It occurred to me it could be the introduction or the first chapter of my dissertation, which could turn out to be a novel or a collection of short stories, or some sort of hybrid text combining essays and short stories. The episode was emblematic; it marked the moment when I began to live with a certain degree of confidence in my new language. Over time, that new language began to take the place of the first, an inevitable transition under the circumstances. With Dad, we always spoke in Spanish, but our conversations were about the everyday; if we delved into something, I would often get lost, and the help he offered me, new vocabulary, words, and expressions, for example, was not enough for me. In the Catholic school where I went for the last two years of high school (The idea came from my grandfather Gustavo. Dad was against it at first, but my grandfather said he would pay for it.), I took several advanced Spanish classes that helped me, especially with reading, although not enough to thoroughly enjoy the novels by Colombian authors that Dad gave me every birthday. Much to my advantage, my relationship with Ana has been completely in Spanish. Even though Ana's English is flawless, she argued that she couldn't be as natural as in Spanish. Thanks to that I've returned to live in my native tongue.

As I walked north on Fifth Avenue, I could smell the scents of Spring, the trees and shrubs were blooming in Central Park. Last year, Ana took selfies for us under the cherry blossoms when we celebrated our first anniversary. Ana is very conventional when it comes to certain celebrations; I'm not used to that. At home we were very informal; we remembered yes, and we gave each other gifts, but we didn't do anything formal; zero ceremony, as Dad says. With Ana, we have to do something out of the ordinary, usually expensive, though that doesn't seem to matter to her: a romantic weekend out of town in an exclusive hotel, a dinner in a good restaurant, or the like; not to mention the formal attire that we must wear.

When I got to the Met, I decided on an itinerary. I would see some of Dad's favorite artworks, which little by little have also become some of my favorites: *The Alchemist*, an engraving by Brueghel the elder, depicting the alchemist working at his stove and three women behind him doing other chores; *a Man in Oriental Costume*, an oil painting of a bearded Ottoman man wearing a turban by Rembrandt, a portrait that Dad jokingly used to say was of a distinguished ancestor, and to prove it, he would stand in profile in front of the painting and groom his short goatee (after many years of playing that charade, I told Dad that it was getting old and I begged him to give it up); and several Renaissance Italian paintings, which he always examined at close range, like someone looking for flaws. Then, I would go through the medieval furniture section, which connected to the 17th-century Spanish paintings gallery, where Goya's work was exhibited. It had been a long time since I had seen it; in my past visits with Ana, we only visited the collection of ancient Greek and Roman art, a subject that fascinated her as she did her undergraduate degree in Classical Studies.

As I walked through the halls, I remembered that, on another occasion, perhaps around the same time that I started to "loosen my tongue," I asked Dad whether Diego Velazquez, the artist whose portraits also caught my attention, could be from our family; after all that was Mom's last name, my second. Dad chuckled, hinting it wouldn't be a shocker, though he later made it clear that it was unlikely and gave me a peculiar look. That afternoon Dad told Mom about it, and she said, "Why not? It would be worth finding out." Although her tone indicated to me that she was making a joke.

In the Spanish paintings gallery, I took a seat on one of the sofas and contemplated the portrait that, as a child, captivated me so much. I saw myself looking curiously at that painting that day I got lost in the museum. Something made me blink, and when I looked at the painting again, I saw Dad in it. That boy's withdrawn gaze was like his the last day I saw him.

TEN

After class, I saw that I had a message from Tía Astrid. She said: "I found out something important, look at this, we need to talk." I brought my laptop to the library and opened the attachment. It was photos of two printed pages from the art section of a Colombian weekly magazine, an article titled, "RAFAEL RUIZ, ARTIST, BOTANIST AND ADVENTURER," published in 1947. On each page, there were six photos, three at the top, and three at the bottom. One of the pictures was of the artist, an older man, tall, bald, and stocky, with one of his sons, a skinny boy dressed in shorts and a woolen sweater, in front of the door of his house. The others were from some of his works, jewelry boxes, and small tables. Tía Astrid had similar pieces in her apartment. I looked at the date again and realized that it couldn't be my grandfather, Dad's father, the dates did not match. I looked at the caption and found out that the boy was also named Rafael Ruiz. The boy was my grandfather; the older man, my great-grandfather. That was my true lineage. In my notebook, I figured out the approximate dates of births:

Rafael Ruiz, great-grandfather, 1890?
Rafael Ruiz, grandfather, 1935?
Magazine article, 1947

Gustavo Herrera, Dad, 1959
Me, 1983

I enlarged the photo of my adventurer great-grandfather and his son, my grandfather, and I opened on my mobile a selfie that my father and I took the day I graduated from college. Three tall men and a boy who would also be tall, judging by the proportions of his arms and legs. Three of them were light-skinned and one a little darker: me; I inherited my skin tone from Mom and her family. I wanted to enlarge the photo to study the faces, but the images were printed on old yellowed newsprint. Up close, they became grainy and blurry. Still, I could make out bushy eyebrows and almond-shaped eyes, just like Dad and I.

The writing in the article was sharp and elegant. There were several sections with suggestive subtitles. The first, "Authentic environment," was a description of the artist's, "workshop-laboratory-home," located in an old colonial neighborhood of Bogotá. The companion photograph reminded me of the engraving, *The Alchemist* by Brueghel the elder, the one Dad often contemplated at the Met. The next one, "Frames and bargueños," was a short history of Taracea art, "the result of Arab influence in Spain and part of what is known as Mudéjar or Mozárabe art." As I read, I thought of how little I knew about Colombian culture. Later on, there was an odd description of the artist who seemed to the author like, "Saint Joseph working in his shop," something that made me think of the nativity scene that Mom made for Christmas, a custom that Dad and I continued for a few years after she passed, though without her effervescent and contagious enthusiasm. The next section,

"Adventures," consisted of several paragraphs with a literary bent about the artist's adventures in southern Colombia and his apprenticeship in botany. It seems my great-grandfather learned on his own. He invented his own system for classifying herbs and fungi and experimented on himself in search of ways of curing different ailments. The final section, titled, "The Clients," barely two paragraphs, made it clear that his clients were wealthy people of renown.

When I finished reading, I called Tía Astrid.

"What did you think?" she asked.

"My great-grandfather was quite a character."

"He had thirteen children, eight of whom survived," Tía Astrid stressed in a tone of amazement.

"How many descendants do you think?"

"I'll start researching tomorrow. I have a lawyer friend who can help me find that family."

"What did you think of his adventures?" she asked.

"They're unbelievable, literally."

"On a government website, I confirmed that in that southern province that borders the Amazon rainforest, there was a penal colony for convicts of fraud crimes that opened at the end of the 19th century. But the dates don't add up. The article suggests that he was there for over ten years, but that colony was shut down in the early 1920s."

"Unless the convict was his father and his mother had passed," I ventured.

"Or that he lied about his age. Perhaps instead of fifty, which he said he was, he was sixty, that is, he was born at the end of the 1890s."

"Or he was playing a prank on the reporter or journalist."

"Could be," Tía Astrid said.

"In any case, it was down there in the South where he supposedly learned botany."

"Although he could have learned that in any other region." "That he cured himself of leprosy, paralysis, and tuberculosis is hard to believe, they are not minor illnesses," I noted.

"The same that it was he who invented and prepared the *menjurje* concoctions."

"I haven't heard the word menjurje for a long time."

"One of your dad's favorite words. As a child, he liked the sound of it, and he repeated it over and over again. The other day I brought him a mixed tropical fruit juice, and when he tasted it he said, this menjurje is delicious."

"How was he, by the way?"

"In good spirits. He was watching a soccer game."

"Did he say something to you?" I asked, and in my mind, saw Dad sitting on the edge of the couch at home watching a soccer game; he is a fan of several Colombian teams and of every European team that had Colombian players on its roster. Sometimes I would sit with him to watch a game, especially if it was a European club final or the World Cup.

"No. He asked me about you, and I told him you were fine."

"Did you tell him something about the botanist and adventurer Rafael Ruiz?"

"No. And not about the other Rafael Ruiz, his own father, either. The doctor who sees him at the nursing home told me that it was not a good idea at the moment. I'm going to discuss it with his neurologist next week."

"Did you talk to your friend the restorer?" I asked.

"Yes. He told me that he didn't know Rafael Ruiz personally, but he knew who he was. It seems that at one time he was a well-known artisan and restorer. Someone told him that he was from a town in the Lowlands, two or three hours from Bogotá, but he did not know the name of the town or the province. He promised me that he would inquire with his colleagues. Then he told me something quite interesting, you'll see. We started talking about antiques and he told me that the man who stole the bargueño from your father, this Rosiñol del Valle, had returned to Bogotá and tried to scam some collectors with some furniture he claimed were antiques, the old trick of giving you a pig in a poke. According to my friend, this Rosiñol del Valle, who now calls himself Carlos Cárdenas, went around several countries –Colombia, Ecuador, Perú and México– buying and selling furniture and antiques. The Bogotá collectors unmasked him by pure chance. One of them was a friend of a Jesuit art historian, a specialist in colonial furnishings. When he examined one of the works Rosiñol del Valle or Cárdenas was selling, the Jesuit realized that they were hybrid pieces, which had original parts from the 16th century and new ones from more recent periods, all of it carefully restored, perhaps by himself."

"A pirate restorer," I said.

Tía Astrid laughed and said, "Francisco, I see the *pirata* thing is going on. Does Annie keep calling you that?"

She sometimes tells me things that I don't understand. The other day she told me, "Pánfilo, you didn't tell me the story of the bargueño," 'and I had no clue what she meant.'"On the net, I saw that it was a name, but that didn't help; she meant something else."

"Didn't you ask her?"

"No. As I told you before if I ask her about something that I don't understand, she makes fun of me and she tells me: "See, that's why you have to take Colombian Spanish classes."

"It is a term of endearment. Pánfilo in that context means silly. Don't take it the wrong way."

"Like when Mom would say to Dad, "You're so silly" and kissed him?"

"Something like that."

"Give Annie a hug from me. I would like to meet her in person. Why don't you come with her to Bogotá this summer?"

"I don't know. It depends on how I do with my exams."

"Ah! You're always taking exams. But I understand you, Francisco. Don't worry. Back to the matter of the former thief, now pirate restorer. You won't guess where he lives now," she said as if it were a question.

"No idea Tía," I replied.

"In New York! Go figure! My friend says he was told that the address on his business card is in Long Island City, in Queens. Practically in Astoria. My friend is going to get me the exact address. As soon as he has it, I'll send it to you. Perhaps that scoundrel can shed more light on Rafael Ruiz.

After all, he returned the stolen bargueño to him. An interesting enigma, don't you think?"

ELEVEN

While searching the Internet for Carlos Cárdenas, New York, I found a few surprises. I found his name on the web pages of three organizations serving the Colombian community in New York; also Dad's, and D'Artagnan's, Emilio Agudelo, his actual name. The first was from the Colombian Chamber of Commerce in New York, where the three appeared on a list of over two hundred business owners and managers of Colombian companies and small businesses in the metropolitan area, also including parts of New Jersey. It was to be expected that all three were listed there. There was nothing unusual. Cárdenas's business, Altamira Fine Art, was located in Long Island City, Queens, confirming what Tía Astrid had told me. From the address, I knew I was on the border with Astoria, an industrial area where I went jogging on the weekends, back when I was in high school. I clicked on the link and it took me to a "Page under construction" announcement. I went back to the previous page looking for a phone number or an email, but there was nothing.

The second, "Colombian Pride," the most intriguing, seemed to be nothing else but a Facebook page without any information other than that it was a non-profit organization, created in 2016, two years ago. I found all three names on the list of over twelve hundred followers. The cover photo was a Colombian flag, a symbol that without any context could mean anything. The main section was filled with links and pictures taken from the Culture section of a Bogota newspaper's Sunday edition.

The third, related to the first, was an article titled: "The Colombian Chamber of Commerce, a model entity for the immigrant community in New York." in an interdisciplinary scientific journal of humanities and social sciences, "Cuadernos Colombianos," published by the "Association of Colombianistas."All three names – again in the context of business owners and managers – appeared in an appendix, a listing of those who had provided information for the article. I read the text with interest; the author was a sociologist of Colombian origin who taught at one of the city's public universities. It was primarily a narrative about the origin of CCC in the sixties, its development over time, and an analysis of data that suggested the progress of some of its affiliated companies. I found it curious that the methodology section mentioned, in-depth interviews, because in the text there was no voice other than the author's. In the end, it concluded, apart from what the title already announced, that it was a "dynamic entity that promoted Colombian businesses, as well as Colombian culture in general."

As I made myself an instant noodle soup for lunch, I remembered that Dad attended one of the executive committee meetings of the Colombian Chamber of Commerce, at the invitation of his best friend at the time, Tito Cruz, owner of a popular travel agency in Jackson Heights, whom he'd known since we arrived in New York, who was its vice president. He said it was an experience that he did not want to repeat. According to Dad, the topics of conversation exposed the ideological quarrels between the members of the entity, which echoed the political polarization in Colombia. Dad had no patience for Colombian politics, he said that he had enough of the rarefied political climate in the United States, which was the only one that interested him because it was the country where he lived and where he planned to spend the rest of his life. How ironic it was that when his early dementia crept in, which threatened to erase his past, somehow mine as well, he decided to return to Colombia.

As if by reflex, I opened the photo application on my computer and looked at the file of photos of my high school graduation day, in June 2000. That afternoon Dad and I attended, as guests of honor, a party at Tito Cruz's house in Long Island. Angela, his eldest daughter, was also graduating. She was one of my classmates and a good friend. Although Dad always denies it, he would have liked me to marry her. He knew her well, we studied together at home one or two days a week throughout high school; we were inseparable at school parties and events, we even had our first kiss together and a brief romance that didn't work out. Cruz was separated from his wife, who had returned to Colombia with his other two younger daughters. According to Angela, he was considerate and affectionate, but old-fashioned. He expected everyone at home to defer to his authority and behave in a way he thought proper. To make matters worse, despite the twenty-odd years that he had been in New York, he still didn't speak English well and Angela didn't like to speak Spanish – her level was terrible. I helped her with it, we took those classes together.

The party was attended by the executive members of the Colombian Chamber of Commerce and their children, those who were our age or a little younger. That whole afternoon reminded me of the wedding party scene in the first *The Godfather* movie. Cruz hired a catering service with uniformed waiters in bowties, and a Latin band of half a dozen musicians to liven up the afternoon in the backyard. All the guests, young and old, wore formal clothes: jacket and tie for boys and men, party dresses for girls and women: it was the norm in these types of gatherings, despite the early June heat. Cruz went from table to table greeting and toasting with the guests, who treated him with a deference that seemed exaggerated to me as if he were pulling the strings of their lives. One of them, a middle-aged man, paunchy and bald, whom Dad told me owned several small businesses in Brooklyn, said aloud, to everyone, that Cruz was a paragon of virtues, something that neither Angela nor I understood, we had never heard that expression in Spanish.

After the meal they served –Valencian paella, fruit and vegetable salads– the musicians played salsa and merengue songs, and the parents started to dance. Angela and I and some of the kids our age went down to the basement of the house where there was a large game room, with a pool table and video game consoles, decorated with framed posters promoting tourism to Colombia, landscapes Andean, and the Caribbean, also flowers and fruits. At some point, one of the boys, the son of the bald and pot-bellied man, rolled a joint that we all shared. Angela put on music, I remember it was an Avril Lavigne album, and after a few minutes, we all started dancing, though not necessarily to the music. The joint had quite a punch, and some of us were throwing arms this way and that, singing out of tune or the like. The adults realized what was happening and came down to the basement. The photos I have of that moment were taken by a friend that Angela and I had in common, who was a year behind us at school. In one of them, Dad was smiling knowingly. Cruz, on the other hand, has a grimace of surprise or perhaps horror on his face. The expressions of the other adults, three or four, cover the median ranges. Despite the interruption, the celebration went on like nothing had happened. Dad told me later that between him and others, they convinced Cruz to let us enjoy our fun, after all the party was in our honor. Back home that night, Dad and I discussed the joint incident: I assured him that I didn't smoke often and that I didn't use any other drugs. Also, that I hadn't slept with Angela, we were both virgins. It was perhaps the first time that Dad and I talked man to man. I guess it was his way of telling me that I was old enough to make my own decisions.

    I didn't see Angela again for several years. According to Dad, Cruz convinced her to go to Colombia to live with her mother. The last I heard from her was that she had married an expatriate gringo in Colombia. The world goes round and round.

    I looked back at the, "Colombian Pride," Facebook page sensing that there was something there that I was not seeing.

I also didn't quite understand what the expression meant. In my reading, it could be at least two things: a kind of *tozudez*, that is, bullheadedness, one of Dad's favorite words; or the collective achievements of an entire country.

TWELVE

D'Artagnan brought us a bottle of aged rum for after dinner. It was Dad's birthday and we always celebrated with a special dinner, usually a seafood casserole that he made himself. Mom started the custom when we moved to New York, so in a way it was also the anniversary of the beginning of our new life. That night, Ana also prepared a seafood soup, though Japanese style, a dish that she learned from a cousin of hers who lived in Tokyo for several years. To enjoy the fresh air and the view of the East River and the full moon, we set the table parallel to the balcony and opened its doors wide. A bottle of Riesling rested in a bucket of ice.

"Cheers, dear old man," D'Artagnan said and raised his glass.

Ana looked at me somewhat surprised.

"Cheers, Dad," I said.

Ana smiled and toasted with us.

"I spoke to Dad this morning," I said. He remarked that he was worried about the news from the United States, he had a feeling that the Republican candidate was going to win the elections. Then he asked me how my relationship with Ana was going. I told him, manna from heaven, and to my delight it made him laugh. He said, 'I'm truly glad'. I told him that she was making dinner tonight. He said, 'Good, though it's a pity that D'Artagnan can't join you.' I told him that he was coming and explained that the bartender he hired was going to cover for him. Dad was silent for a moment, and then said, a little unsure of himself, of course, he just arrived in New York. Then he told me again for the umpteenth time the story of how he became partners with his best friend, Emilio Agudelo to save the bankrupt antique store in Bogotá.

"My father," D'Artagnan clarified.

"The only difference, I continued, was that this time he said something I didn't know: that your father was my grandfather Gustavo's lawyer, who did the paperwork for his adoption. My biological grandfather Rafael Ruiz told him. Did you know that D'Artagnan?"

"No, but it doesn't surprise me," he replied in a meditative tone. "My dad and your grandfather were close friends from their college days. They had total confidence in each other. When my dad passed away, your grandfather Gustavo was the executor of his will. From then on, he took care of our finances. My mom was very grateful; poor thing, she was just beginning her teaching career at the university, and she just didn't have enough time for anything.

"And was it then that you came to New York for the first time," Ana asked.

"A couple of years later, after I finished college," he replied. "I came here because I needed to leave Colombia, I felt suffocated there. It was a difficult time because my mother remarried a Chilean political exile, a guy who had many psychological problems, sequels of the torture he endured when he was an active member of the Communist

Youth brigades in Santiago. He made my life impossible. I didn't get along with him. We argued all the time –not about politics, we were more or less on the same page on that– but about our everyday life. He didn't like the arrangement that Mom and Grandpa Gustavo made about the family's finances. He wanted to be in control of the money; he wanted to buy a better car, go on holiday to Cartagena for Christmas, and so on. But his salary as a copyeditor at a university press was not enough for those luxuries. He also liked to go out with his friends, he loved partying; at the end of the month, he hardly ever had a peso left. Mom gave him some money from time to time, though nearly every time told him to be measured and to remember his principles. Thanks to Mom's discipline, we were able to finance my trip to New York and there was enough money left to pay the lawyer who helped me get my green card."

"Francisco told me that the lawyer got someone to marry you," Ana said that with a knowing smile.

"Yes, that's how it was. I didn't want to be undocumented anywhere, I wanted to be free, travel, and see the world, but with a Colombian passport it was difficult in the nineties; now less so. The woman I married for the papers, a Puerto Rican painter, also wanted to travel, so a few months after I got the residency permit, after two years and three months –the time I worked in the store with Gustavo in Jackson Heights– we went to Europe together; that was in June of ninety-nine. In Barcelona, we met some Dutch backpackers who were traveling through several countries selling wire handicrafts that they made themselves. They invited me to join them and I accepted. The Puerto Rican painter stayed in Barcelona, I think she still lives there. Needless to say, that was the perfect excuse for our divorce."

"I don't see you backpacking," Ana commented, raising her eyebrows, her tone flush with irony.

"Neither do I," I said. "If you'll forgive me, your style has always been of a dandy. How did you manage to go backpacking?"

D'Artagnan hummed a song.

"I don't get it."

"It's an old Colombian song about having been young and carefree, Francisco," Ana said. "Your Colombian identity lost ten points tonight! But tell us your whole story, D'Artagnan. Warts and all. You promised us before, she reminded him."

"There is not much to tell, but since you insist, I'll continue. From Barcelona, we went to Madrid, Brussels, Paris, Rome, Frankfurt, and Berlin. In each city, we stayed for two weeks. Generally, we did well, earning about two hundred dollars per day. Each of us sold our wares in a different place in the city and we rotated every other day. Our overhead was low; we stayed in youth hostels or camping parks, traveling in an old Volkswagen van. There were eight of us, the six Dutch, a Venezuelan musician, and me. Our final destination was Istanbul, where the plan was to hang out for the rest of the summer, and then return to Spain. The Dutch were students of Hispanic Philology at the University of Salamanca, and the semester began in September. César, the Venezuelan, and I decided to continue traveling; we both wanted to go to Prague and Budapest and perhaps Warsaw. To cover our expenses, César suggested that we sell our wares during the day and do a music show at night: he on guitar, I on percussion; in Brussels I'd bought an acoustic cajón at a flea market and had learned to play alongside César, who liked to sing *nueva trova* songs during our long road trips."

"You gave us the itinerary of the journey, D'Artagnan, but not the juicy details," Ana said feigning a scolding. "What did you do when you weren't working? Did you go out and party? Did you meet people, did you fall in love? Tell us!"

"I'll need some rum for that", D'Artagnan said. "But don't expect anything extraordinary."

By then we had finished dinner. Ana and I picked up the dishes and dimmed the lights. A light breeze came from the river and the distant murmur of city traffic. Ana opened the bottle of rum and poured us glasses.

"Well, I did meet someone with whom I fell in love," D'Artagnan said and took a sip of his rum. It was in Prague that I met Anezka, my wife; my ex-wife. César had a somewhat eccentric Andalusian friend, à la Salvador Dalí, with a thin mustache bent at the ends, his hair slicked back, who taught at a language school and had a somewhat dilapidated apartment with large bedrooms overlooking the Vltava River. We stayed there for a few days. The guy was older than us, maybe forty, but he acted like he was twenty years younger. He made a joke about everything, he just wanted to have fun. Everybody called him Rooks but that wasn't his real name, and to my recollection, nobody knew it. He hardly ever spent time at the apartment; he had several girlfriends, some of them his students. One night he had a party, and to my surprise, he played Colombian tropical music, cumbias, and vallenatos. Because of his way of dancing, I thought he had learned in Colombia, although sometimes he overdid the steps and moved his hips in a somewhat comical way, like Cantinflas in old Mexican movies. When I asked him half-jokingly what part of Colombia he was from, he paid me in the same coin. 'It's a well-kept secret,' he said and laughed. He added confidently that Anezka, one of his students, a nice redhead that I had met a couple of days ago, had been staring at me for quite a while, and I should ask her to dance. At that moment, I realized that his Andalusian accent was fake. Something in the way he spoke, and his word choices told me that he was from Bogotá, but I didn't say anything. I was reminded of this recently, though I am not entirely sure of the order in which things happened; I'll tell you why later. The fact is, the next morning I found myself in Anezka's bed, in her apartment, not knowing how I got there. When I opened my eyes, I saw her smiling, saying good morning to me. I was surprised for an instant, but for some reason, I didn't feel anything negative; neither fear nor shame. I felt happy. I figured that I would remember last night little by little before long. Anezka said that I should feel at home and suggested we have a coffee. From the kitchen, I realized that we were in the upper part of the city, in an old neighborhood near the Castle and Saint Vitus Cathedral. We talked about the master's thesis in journalism that she was writing on the political and economic project of the European Union. After a while, she told me: 'We can go whenever you want to collect your things.' I laughed, I thought it was a joke but I could tell from Anezka's face that she was serious. 'I told you the sofa bed was comfortable,' she added, and she blushed slightly. I apologized and said, sure, the sofa bed is fine, and took a sip of coffee to hide my surprise. Anezka said that she was going to take a shower and reminded me that I should feel at home. I remember the moment Anezka came out of the kitchen I felt that somehow everything was falling into place. From one moment to another, my life was taking an unmistakably clear turn; the mechanism of the universe favored me. The absurd idea that Anezka and I had been a couple in the distant past occurred to me, perhaps in another life. That night, after dinner and under the pleasant buzz of a few drinks, we danced boleros, cumbias, and gaitas from the fifties that I had recorded onto a cassette tape. Anezka's steps were smooth and steady and instinctively followed mine. I know it sounds silly, but understanding myself on the dance floor with a partner is a sign of compatibility, especially in bed. Later, after making love, she told me that the press agency for which she worked was going to open an office in Paris, and she was part of the team to set it up so she would have to go in a couple of weeks. I told her Paris was my destination and proposed that we go together. I've never been so daring in my life! But I did not doubt that this was what I was going to do, what I *had* to do. Anezka looked at me with a mixture of surprise and tenderness and said: 'Why not? We'll see how it goes.'

The rest of the story you already know: fifteen years of marriage to a wonderful woman, a friendly, if not perfect, divorce, and a beautiful fifteen-year-old, Pascale, my daughter who is coming to New York this summer."

THIRTEEN

D'Artagnan downed the rest of the rum from his glass in one swift gulp, his gaze fixed on the East River, in the distance. An airplane, a mere shadow with wingtips lights blinking like a distant constellation, was making its descent towards La Guardia Airport on the opposite shore. By a strange coincidence, Ana and I crossed our arms simultaneously.

"Your story is quite the revelation," Ana said, breaking the brief pause. "Did you ever recall what happened at the party?"

"No, the memory eluded me, and I hesitated to ask Anezka that morning–or in the days that ensued. For some reason, I feared upsetting her. After a week or two, when our relationship felt more secure, I confessed my lack of recollection about that first night. She found it amusing, laughing it off. 'The party was lively, and we danced the night away. However, when we got into bed ready to make love, you promptly succumbed to sleep,' she teased. Then, with her eyes locked onto mine, perhaps slightly impatient with my innocence, she unveiled the truth. 'It was those space brownies laced with marijuana, a gift from your compatriot. He casually remarked, 'Eat two, you need to relax,' or something of the sort, and you devoured them in no time.'"

"Wow," Ana exclaimed. "I would have been furious with that guy, I would have reported him to the police! Just imagine if you'd had a bad trip."

"He put your life in danger," I chimed in.

"I was actually grateful," D'Artagnan said.

"That he put your life in danger?" Ana raised an eyebrow.

"That marked the beginning of a new stage in my life," D'Artagnan replied and took a sip of rum.

"A new stage born from a blackout," Ana quipped.

"What marks a beginning is irrelevant, what matters is what unfolds. From that day forward, something within me, at the core of me, started to change. Gradually, I realized that nothing tethered me, and the entire world lay before me—I could venture in any direction with anyone I pleased."

"I'm not sure I grasp it," Ana admitted, resting an elbow on the table with her hand supporting her cheek. "I understand how a romance can alter your life, but this core change is a bit elusive."

"Perhaps 'core' is not the most fitting term. I don't know how to explain it. At times, I feel it's intertwined with language—the very fabric of our communication. When I learned English in Colombian classrooms and here in New York, I remained unchanged, a mere translation. Yet, in French—the language woven into my life with Anezka and Pascal, the language that enveloped my mornings, afternoons, and nights—I underwent a gradual metamorphosis into someone entirely different."

"And now that you're in New York, did you go back to your old self?" I asked and thought of Dad the day he returned to Colombia when something in him was already changing. At the airport, I told him: 'Bye Dad and he reacted in the way he always did when he heard me say that; he couldn't help it, he translated me in his own way. He would say, don't say bye; say, see you later; I will always see you later; goodbye does not imply that certainty.'

"That's no longer possible, Francisco," D'Artagnan replied. "I don't think I could even if I tried."

"Let's toast to your new life; you're lucky it turned out so well," Ana said, and served us another round of rum.

"What I don't understand is why you returned to New York," I noted. "You could have stayed in France or another part of Europe. Dad tried to explain that to me but he couldn't. He wasn't sure if it was a business matter or something personal. I told him to forget about it, it didn't matter; by then he had already realized that his memory was failing."

"Because I no longer saw myself in Paris," D'Artagnan replied, drumming his fingers on the table. "Let's say that that part of my life came to an end. Once Anezka and I decided to divorce, the only thing that tied me to Paris, to France, was Pascale. But I secretly knew that Pascale wanted to study in New York; she had told me several times, so I said to myself, in two years my daughter will be in New York, not to mention that she will spend the summers that remain with me."

"Wow. You're going very fast," Ana observed. "There's a big gap between a romance in Prague and a divorce in Paris. How did you get the visas and residence permits? What did you do to make a living?"

"It wasn't easy," D'Artagnan replied and scratched his temple. "The paperwork was unbelievably complicated but thanks to that my French improved. In the Spring of the following year, Pascale was born. I still didn't have a stable job, I taught English and Spanish at a language school in *Quartier Latin*. At night, I worked as a disc jockey in a nightclub, in the same neighborhood. After a year, the owner couple, a French woman and a Mexican guy, proposed that I work full time and join their business partnership. That made all the difference; I was finally able to support my family and save some money."

"Did you ever think of going back to Colombia?" Ana asked.

"Sure, but I had no reason to go back. It may sound strange, but after being out of Colombia for four or five years, I was certain that I was never going to return. I never felt nostalgic for the country or its culture or its food or anything. I guess over time it became a place like any other. When I lived in Paris, I felt nostalgic for my life in New York; that's why I came back here, I think this is my true home." D'Artagnan was going to add something but thought better of it and fell silent.

Ana cleared her throat before commenting:

"I don't understand how you can have such certainty, such rejection for your own country. I don't think I could ever say that, and I've been out for eight years now."

"But I don't think you've ever really left," I noted. "You're always worried about what happens in Colombia; you are very invested in its politics, in its culture, in everything."

"Invested?"

"Francisco means that you follow very closely everything that happens in Colombia."

"Thanks *a lot,* D'Artagnan," I said.

"I understood what you said, don't think I'm dull-witted," Ana snapped. "I understand the nuance of "investing" in this case, though I don't think it's good usage. And, it's true, I closely follow everything that happens in Colombia, but it is precisely because that is my country, my home, my frame of reference."

"But you prefer to live in New York," I pointed out.

"New York is something else; here it's not difficult to be Colombian. It is also a city where you find whatever you want. But if you don't mind, I'd like to change the subject. There is something I have always wanted to know about your transformation, D'Artagnan: who gave you the nickname?"

"Didn't you tell her, Francisco?"

"I always assumed it was Dad, he finds nicknames for everyone; except for me; I would not allow it."

"It was Anezka," D'Artagnan beamed. "One fine day she told me: 'your name doesn't fit your personality, you're a D'Artagnan,' and from that day forward, that's what she called me. I had to read Dumas's book on the sly, I was ashamed to admit that I didn't know what she meant. The night Pascale was born, Anezka called the club to let me know that she was on her way to the hospital, she had broken her water, and busy as she was instead of using my name, she asked about D'Artagnan."

Ana burst out a giggle.

"What a great story," I said. "Does Pascale call you that?"

"She has never called me Dad, much less, Emilio."

"It fits you perfectly," Ana commented.

D'Artagnan made a theatrical bow, and for some reason, the three of us stared into the distance on the other side of the East River towards the glow of the Queens neighborhoods sprawled to the horizon.

"And what happened to César and the Spanish-Colombian guy?" I asked. Something on the horizon had made me think of the guy with the thin mustache bent at the ends, his hair slicked back.

"You must be a mind reader," he replied. "I was getting there, Francisco. The world goes round and round. I didn't see César again, but I found him on Facebook and we are now friends, although we haven't exchanged more than a few greetings. He lives in Tokyo and runs a bar, or he owns it; I'm not sure, he doesn't say either way on his page. It's funny that our lives took such parallel tracks. What's surprising is that in the photos he posted he looks exactly as I knew him, lanky, haggard, his long hair tied in a ponytail, although already all gray, like mine. With Carlos Cárdenas it was different. I didn't know that that was his last name until recently. One day, he showed up at the bar and said: 'Hello, Emilio, long time no see.' I looked at him from head to toe, I didn't recognize him, though his somewhat formal attire, jacket, waistcoat, and tie, and his slicked-back hair seemed vaguely familiar; I thought he was a classmate from high school or college, only they would call me by my first name. I told him

I didn't remember him and he told me: 'But Emilio, how are you going to forget that night when you hooked up with one of the students from the language school in Prague! I found out that you went with her to Paris.' I thought about it for a moment and to my mind came that first meeting with Anezka, the night of the party in Prague, the moment I took her out to dance; I saw it in my mind in slow motion. Anezka had her pageboy hair dyed red, was wearing all black, and had on a pair of Dr. Martens boots. A vallenato song by Jorge Oñate was playing, and we began to dance. From there, everything fades away. The next thing was her eyes and her good morning in bed."

"Carlos Cárdenas is Rosiñol del Valle," I said, perhaps a bit too loud. Ana and D'Artagnan looked at me in surprise.

"Rosiñol del Valle, the one who stole the bargueño from your father?" D'Artagnan asked in a kind of whisper.

"The very same. The man himself," I added.

"I can't believe you!"

"Me neither."

"The restorer of antiques?" Ana asked.

"Ninety-eight percent."

"Do you know how to find him?" I asked D'Artagnan.

"He gave me his business card, I have it in the office. Tomorrow morning when I'm at the bar I'll text you the address."

"But why did he come to your bar?" asked Ana.

D'Artagnan crossed his arms and wrinkled his brow. "He told me that he had found me on the list of the Colombian Chamber of Commerce; he was also a member, and he owned a furniture factory in Queens. He didn't give me any particulars, and I didn't ask; you know how I am, always with my guard up. He said that he wanted to propose a deal that would benefit both of us. He suggested using my bar to promote and sell Colombian arts and crafts, mentioning emerald jewelry, fine woolen and cotton fabrics, and leather goods. Without my saying anything, he commented that we would have to redecorate, put two or three display cases for the items for sale, and change the concept from a Parisian bar to Colombian folklore. I told him I wasn't interested in either idea. Yet, he didn't give up. He pointed out that the location in the Village was perfect, arguing that in this part of the city, there was a very liberal audience: artists, writers, academics, and graduate students who liked or claimed to like ethnic and folksy stuff, considering their consumption politically correct, part of their identity as enlightened citizens of the world, defenders of diversity and human rights. To be honest, his attempt at seduction made me falter for a moment. I managed to imagine some of my clients—who, I hate to say, are more or less like the clientele he outlined—buying the merchandise from us. Some would prefer items in the Andean line, peasant poncho ruanas and hats, woolen scarves and sweaters in bright colors and designs; at night they would come to the bar to listen to string music, *bambucos,* and *torbellinos*. Others would prefer the Tropical Passion line, *vueltiao* straw hats, guayaberas, and multicolored hammocks; at night they would come to listen to traditional *porro, gaita, and vallenato* music."

D'Artagnan paused in his monologue. The three of us looked towards the river at the same time; a tugboat was sailing fast towards the sea, its distant engine purring in the night.

"I told him again that I wasn't interested," D'Artagnan went on. "Then Cárdenas looked at his wristwatch and said: 'I fancy a gin and tonic. Hendrick's, if you have it, consider me a customer.'

"As soon as I poured him the drink, he began to tell me the story of his life; he gave me the impression that he was a very lonely man. He said that he was the adopted son of a Dutch couple in Bogotá who died in a plane crash in the late 1980s when he was beginning his degree in Linguistics at university. After he got his degree, he landed a job with the Federation of Colombian Coffee Growers, and thanks to his ease with languages –he spoke English and Dutch fluently, and had a good command of Japanese, it was one of the languages he majored in–he got transferred, first to the New York office and, after five years, to the Tokyo office, located in the commercial section of the Colombian embassy. After six or seven months in Japan, he married a Japanese nurse, a student of his in a salsa class that he taught on weekends at a nightclub. Thanks to his knowledge of Japanese culture and customs, he was appointed head of cultural affairs the following year. To supplement his civil servant salary, he entered into a partnership with some Latin American immigrants and started a Latino restaurant club in an entertainment area in Tokyo, which according to him was a success. Unfortunately, after five years, the pace of work and the collapse of his marriage took its toll on him and he decided to sell his part of his business and return to New York, where all his friends and his family lived."

"What a character," Ana remarked.

I nodded got up and poured us one last round of rum.

FOURTEEN

Professor Rodrigues was on the phone and motioned for me to take a seat. He continued his lively conversation about a manuscript that he was translating or editing, I couldn't figure out which. He spoke English with an Australian accent that reminded me of my time in London as an exchange student. There, I formed a short but close friendship with an Australian professor who taught World Cinema, and his wife, a journalist and culture columnist. We spent afternoons discussing films at a pub in Russell Square, near the university campus. Sometimes, other classmates would join us, and we would all go out to eat, also to dance. We loved going to a Jazz and Blues club in Covent Garden where there was always live music. I had a great time, I loved the city; I never tired of walking down the streets, which reminded me of the many novels I had read since high school and in English literature courses at the university. I've always been a bit of an Anglophile.

"Sorry, I kept you waiting," Rodrigues said, still in English. Like the other day I saw him, he wore a black turtleneck shirt, giving him a vaguely priestly appearance, especially at that Jesuit university uptown. "I'm glad you came," he remarked, switching to Spanish, and his tone took on a different quality. It was the first time I had heard him speak in his native language. His accent echoed that of Dad or my grandfather Gustavo, very *cachaco*, old-fashioned Bogotá style. Despite myself, I smiled with closed lips.

"As I mentioned in the email, it's an honor for me to be invited to join your dissertation committee," he continued, rolling his Rs like my grandfather Gustavo. "My comments on your proposal are handwritten on the copy I printed; I'm a bit old-fashioned about these things. I also prefer in-person meetings to discuss my comments. You'll see that my suggestions are purely bibliographical, mainly for the theoretical section. I would also recommend including, in the methodology section, the personal reasons influencing your decision to work in this manner. It's evident to me that this dissertation is another way of understanding your own life. Once you finish the fieldwork and start writing, feel free to send me individual chapters. I'll gladly offer my impressions and comments."

Rodrigues paused, his brow furrowing slightly. "I noticed in the proposal that you indicated you would read my novel as an example of auto-ethnography. I suppose Vartatian suggested it to you."

I nodded.

"Good luck," he said and smiled. "I don't know if you know that he and I have known each other for more than twenty years."

"I didn't know. Did you go to school together?"

"No, it was before that. We were both backpacking in Java, Indonesia, in the late eighties. One night we met in a restaurant in Yogyakarta, near the Sultan's palace. I was with a young Dutch woman I had met in Malaysia, and he was with Marta Salazar, but they had not yet married, they were classmates at Berkeley. I was on my way to Sydney for my doctorate in history, and Monica, the Dutch girl was doing a dual degree an in Anthropology and History. The place was packed and all four of us were seated at the same table. We were very amused to learn that we all wanted to be academics. Over a few beers, we also discovered that we had similar tastes in literature and film. Interestingly, the four of us had read the recently published first novel by Amitav Ghosh, a young university professor at the time. We talked until dawn, knowing we wouldn't meet again, as we were traveling in opposite directions. We exchanged addresses, but for some reason, we never made contact. If it weren't for finding Marta on Facebook four or five years ago, we wouldn't have seen each other again. Last year, I invited them to a conference on travel literature in Latin America at my university in Tokyo; I am a full-time professor at St. Xavier University."

"Am I keeping you too long?" Rodrigues asked.

"Not at all," I told him. I sensed that he wanted to continue talking about his past, and it intrigued me. Something about Rodrigues was familiar to me; he reminded me of my grandfather Gustavo, not just in his speech and accent but also in his bearing and formal demeanor.

Rodrigues looked me in the eye and blinked suddenly, as if something had irritated his eye. Maybe the heating, the air was very dry.

I asked him about the conference.

"Excellent," he replied and crossed his arms. "The presentations were very good. A group of colleagues and I, who presented on Colombian travel literature, agreed to publish our papers in an edited volume."

"Do you know Colombian travel literature?"

"A little bit," I lied. I felt somewhat uncomfortable: I didn't want to discuss Colombian literature, I did not think I could handle it, much less at an academic level. This was one of my weak points. Though technically, I had no reason to worry—my proposal made no mention of Colombian literature, and it wasn't relevant to my project.

"I'd like to read those papers," I said, remembering that I had read a couple of novels by a Colombian writer set in Beijing and Bangkok, wondering if they qualified as travel literature.

"Let me ask the authors and I'll pass them on to you." Rodrigues was about to add something else, but he stopped and looked at the papers on the desk.

"I hadn't thought about it until now," he said in a low voice, shaking his index finger, another gesture reminiscent of my grandfather Gustavo. "If you write a novel," he continued, "it will be a Latinx novel. I don't like the term at all, by the way. It couldn't be otherwise: you are the child of Latin Americans, and you write about the experience of living as immigrants in this country. At the same time, it is an American novel. Also Colombian, of course."

"If I write it, it would be in English," I said, somewhat dumbfounded.

"There are already authors like you, descendants of Colombian immigrants, whose works are translated into Spanish and are considered works of Colombian literature."

"I never thought about that," I admitted.

"But there is no reason to worry about what those who consider themselves guardians of national literature say," he hastened to add. "Your project is anthropology–Vartatian and I had a long chat about that. If your novel, if this is what you're going to write, is of interest to scholars in literary studies, much the better for you; there will be other doors that would open to you. Then, you'll decide if it works for you or not."

Rodrigues made that last remark in a tone of encouragement.

"By the way, what kind of literature do you like?"

"I like postcolonial literature," I replied. Interestingly, one of my favorite authors is Amitav Gosh.

"Sure, another anthropologist."

"Also younger ones, like Tan Twan Eng, a Malaysian of Chinese origin. He wrote two novels about the Japanese occupation of Penang that I liked."

"Penang is one of my favorite places," Rodrigues said and leaned back in his chair. "A few years ago, I wrote about the arrival of the Portuguese to that island from Goa, India, in the sixteen century. Over time it became a very important entrepôt in the region. By chance, I've read the novels you mention, and I also like him as a writer. Have you been to Penang?"

"No," I said surprised, and thought of my old Japanese girlfriend, who knew that region well. For me so far away, it was she who recommended that Malaysian author to me.

"And in Spanish?"

"In Spanish," I echoed, still thinking of my Japanese girlfriend and the images I'd made in my mind of that Malaysian island from the two novels: a melting pot of races and cultures, part of the British Empire, in the crosshairs of Japanese imperialism.

"What authors do you like in that language?"

"I don't have favorites, but for obvious reasons, I prefer Colombian authors," I said, a statement that concealed the fact that I knew very little about other literatures in Spanish. I was going to add some names, but I stopped, thinking it was better to leave things as they were.

FIFTEEN

Rodrigues handed me the hard copy of my proposal and reminded me that his comments were on the last page. Leaning back in his chair, he suggested I email him if I had any questions.

"Thanks a million," I said, resorting to the Spanish hyperbole for gratitude, a habit picked up from Dad. Before stowing it in my backpack, I quickly glanced at his comments. It was mostly a list of suggested readings, with two or three titles that Vartatian had also recommended. I felt a sense of relief, an intuitive certainty that Rodrigues would be an ally.

"Professor Vartatian told me that you inherited a 17th-century colonial bargueño," Rodrigues mentioned, sounding almost like a question.

"That's right," I replied. In that moment, I recalled Vartatian mentioning that he and his wife had a small collection of colonial art pieces. Perhaps Rodrigues shared the same appreciation, if not a collector's fervor."

"Could you send me a photo of it?"

I have some here, I said and opened my mobile's photo app.

Rodrigues looked at the images carefully, zooming in and out several times.

"Very interesting," he commented and took out some large-format photographs from a drawer in his desk.

"Tell me what you think," he said, putting the photos within my reach.

I thought it was a joke. They were of a bargueño exactly like mine with engravings of animals on the drawers, though the central bone plate had an engraving not of a bearded man with a turban but a saint with a cross in his hand.

"Is it an antique?" I asked.

"It's a 17th-century piece that has been restored several times. One of the sides was restored using newer wood, from the early nineteen hundreds."

"My bargueño is also an antique, though from the 1930s."

"Do you have the authentication certificate?"

"At home," I replied and remembered that it was in a box with documents of Dad's on one of my bookshelves.

"Do you know its history?"

"My dad inherited it from my grandfather, it's a family heirloom."

"Was your grandfather Rafael Ruiz?"

"How do you know?"

"Was your great-grandfather also called Rafael Ruiz?"

"Yes," I replied, intrigued by his questions.

"I've been tracking your family for a while."

"Why? I don't understand what you're talking about."

"Sorry. This bargueño," he said looking at the photos, "is also an heirloom inherited by a side of your family that you probably don't know."

"Descendants of Rafael Ruiz?"

Rodrigues nodded.

I pulled my water bottle out of my backpack and took a long sip. "I recently found out about my biological family," I said. "My dad was adopted but he didn't know it; he found out recently."

Rodrigues narrowed his eyes and crossed his arms. "It must have been shocking to receive such news," he said in a measured tone. "For you too, I imagine."

"Yes," I said and felt a lump in my throat.

Behind Rodrigues was one of the campus gardens lined with cherry blossoms. The evening would soon fall, and the sun in the distance was shrouded in orange and red clouds.

"Who are these descendants? Where do they live?"

"One of them, Sara Ruiz, is a professor of Art History from Bogotá who teaches at a university in Madrid. She would be your third cousin. I don't know her personally, but we have been in contact by email. She is coming to New York for the meeting of the Historical Association at the end of May. If you'd like, I could introduce you. The other one, Adriana Ruiz, is an executive at a modeling agency in Dubai; she's your second cousin."

"Do you know her?" I asked in English, code-switching despite myself.

"Yes, I met her in Dubai," he replied also in English. "Last year I was a visiting professor at a university there."

"And did they know Rafael Ruiz, my grandfather?"

"Sara, the oldest, no. Adriana, yes, she was his favorite granddaughter. I could put you two in touch if you'd like. They are researching the life of your biological grandfather and the making of the bargueños; there are very interesting things in the engravings."

"They are taken from a medieval bestiary, according to what my father told me."

"Yes, except for the engraving of the bearded man wearing a turban. A colleague and I found a very similar figure, almost the same, on a 16th-century Mughal miniature, which would suggest a Muslim origin, although it may well be of an Andalusian Jewish philosopher from Muslim Spain. We have seen drawings of two, Maimonides from the thirteenth century and Abravanel from the fifteenth century, that also look the same."

"Do you mean to say that there is a Jewish or Muslim ancestor in my family?"

"It's possible," Rodrigues replied. "You should get in touch with Sara Ruiz. She is doing the genealogical tree of the Ruiz family from the 15th century on, also a genetic registry, with DNA test results."

"Yes, of course," I said and thought about Dad; once he jokingly noted that everyone in his family should have DNA tests, no one looked like anyone else. Poor Dad didn't yet know the truth.

"I'll send you the contact information later."

"Would it be possible to see the actual bargueño? I could go to your place if you don't mind."

"Yes, no problem," I replied. "But what exactly are you looking for?"

"I am not a curator of colonial antiques, far from it; but there is something in the main engraving of your bargueño that intrigues me: the lines of the drawings are very similar to those in the 17th-century piece I mentioned earlier. Engraving bone plates requires a lot of skill and the artisans who do it each have their style, his or her signature, let's say; as in any visual art, of course."

SIXTEEN

Tía Astrid answered on the first ring.

"We're in sync, I was going to call you in a few minutes."

"I found out that I have two cousins," I said and told her about my meeting with Rodrigues and what he told me about them.

"You have to contact them, Francisco. What you tell me about the possible Jewish or Muslim origin of your family does not seem strange to me. Do you remember my friend Juana Medina? The one that got a Ph.D. in Art History at Brown?"

The image of the woman came to my mind, tall and skinny, with a delicate and expressive face, and thick eyebrows close to each other almost like those of Dr. Vartatian.

"How can I forget, Tía," I replied. "Don't you remember that I fell in love with her when you introduced us?"

"You must have told Gustavo, you didn't tell *me* anything." Tía Astrid's tone was of mock annoyance as if my forgetfulness were some kind of betrayal of our relationship.

"I remember you told me that she didn't get the job at Xavier University."

"Yes, and that has to do with what I'm going to tell you. Juana always suspected that the origin of her family was Moorish, that is, from Spanish Muslims who came to the New World before they were expelled from Spain, just as they did with the Jews in the time of Queen Isabella. If I remember correctly, it was rumored in her family that one of their ancestors, a doctor or a healer, was tortured by the Inquisition in Cartagena in the 16th century; apparently, there were some letters or documents that recorded the incident in the family's archives. As this was a topic related to her research —on the influence of Al Andalus on Ibero-American art— Juana took a DNA test and it came out that she had a good percentage of Berber genetic material from North Africa, mixed with Arabic, Iberian, and also indigenous to the New World."

"This is why she is so gorgeous," I noted.

"Francisco *pillo*, little rascal," Tía Astrid said teasingly. "What happened was that when Juana applied for a position at Xavier's, one of the professors on the hiring committee, a high-ranking Jesuit priest, was against her candidacy, claiming that her specialty and the focus of her research was Islamic art, an area of study that was not a good fit for the research agenda of the department. He cited as evidence an article that she wrote about the Torre mudéjar, an 18th-century brick bell tower in Cali that, according to him, illustrated the shortcomings of such a perspective. That's why she wasn't hired. In any case, it doesn't surprise me that the bargueño might be of Moorish origin."

"Or Jewish," I said. "The bearded man may be an Andalusian Jewish philosopher, either Maimonides or Abravanel."

"Now that you mention it, I'd say you have more of Dustin Hoffman than Omar Shariff," Tía Astrid added once again teasingly. "But joking aside, you have to meet Sara Ruiz."

"And take a DNA test."

"We should do one for your dad, too, to be on the safe side. But, I found out something else. Rafael Ruiz, your great-grandfather, the botanist, did a restoration of a piece from the *Salón de los Bargueños* in the Casa de Nariño, the presidential palace in the 1920s. It was Juana Medina who helped me get the scoop; she is now the main curator of Spanish colonial art at the government's *Museo del Virreinato* and has priority access to the archives of the presidential palace. That was in the twenties. According to what she told me, the file included a note stating that there was no one else in Bogotá at that time who could properly handle the restoration. Juana explained to me that, unlike the Viceroyalty of Perú and New Spain, in México, in New Granada, there were no artisan guilds, and therefore, there was no tradition of learning restoration. Those who restored colonial antiquities learned the trade on their own; although it cannot be ruled out that there were family dynasties of artisans who during colonial times obtained their examination cards or certificates in the Viceroyalty of Peru and opened restoration workshops in Bogotá. Which brings me to the other thing I have to tell you. It turns out that old man Carrizosa knew Rafael Ruiz, son, your grandfather! I called him the same day I spoke with Juana and told him the whole story. He told me: 'Of course, I was a good friend of Rafael Ruiz, you should've asked me before; he and one of his sisters were skilled taracea artisans, and their work was held in very high regard.' According to the old man, he and Rafael Ruiz, your grandfather, were the same age —the sister was older— and they grew up together in the Las Nieves neighborhood. We are talking about the thirties and forties. Apparently, his father, your great-grandfather, the botanist-adventurer in the magazine article, was a member of the theosophy lodge to which the father of the old man Carrizosa also belonged, and for that reason, they were also good friends. Over time the Carrizosa family, which was very wealthy, moved to another part of the city —at that time Bogotá was beginning the transformation that impoverished the downtown and colonial neighborhoods— and he and your grandfather lost contact. Interestingly, they met again in your grandfather Gustavo's antique store, where Manuel, that is the old man's first name, had brought an old bargueño that was a bit damaged and your grandfather Rafael Ruiz was the one who was in charge of doing that sort of restoration work. From then on, they continued to see each other frequently. This is how he found out that Rafael Ruiz had fallen in love with your grandmother Francisca, a love that was not possible due to class differences, and that after his heart was broken he went to live in Tocaima, a town in the warm Lowlands, two hours southwest from Bogotá, where he married and had two children. The old man says that one of them still lives in that town. I bet that son is Adriana's father, your second cousin, the one who lives in Dubai."

"Wasn't Tocaima the town where we had relatives?"

"No, Francisco. " Tía Astrid replied. "The paternal line of the family, that of your grandfather Gustavo, is from a village near Sasaima, also in the warm Lowlands but to the northwest of Bogotá. That family line has a turbulent history, they are wealthy landowners, but they've had political and business quarrels since the end of the 19th century; they spend their time fighting, in person and in court, to this day; I'll tell you the whole story some other time. The patriarch of that family, my grandfather Gustavo, you know that we call him Gustavo Viejo, senior –What a relief that people don't follow that old-fashioned custom of naming the firstborn after the father, you would be at least Gustavo IV–, was an army captain during the War of a Thousand Days. But when it was time to retire, the government rejected his request, claiming that his name did not appear in their files, as if the absence of a document negated his life. My grandfather obtained witnesses, other officers who, under oath and in writing, confirmed that he had been an officer who distinguished himself by his camaraderie and generosity with his subordinates. But even so, the directives of the Ministry of Defense did not accept it and twenty years passed until it was discovered that some files from the time of the war had been lost. Thanks to another request, this time prepared by a lawyer, the government finally granted his pension. With the money they paid him, which was not all they owed him, but all in all, was a small fortune, he came to Bogotá and opened the antique store that your father inherited. It is from that great-grandfather that the bargueño comes. Perhaps you already knew that, but not from the side of his family but from his wife's, my grandmother Solita. Perhaps your father has told you about her; her name was Soledad Herrera. I know very little about her; her family was from Nocaima, one of the oldest towns in Colombia, and also from the Lowlands, northwest of Bogotá, roughly in the same region as Tocaima and Sasaima. They make a neat triangle on a map, though the region is very mountainous and the roads don't follow straight lines. They moved to Bogotá when she was a little girl. Her family was very wealthy; they inherited quite a bit of farmland and a copper mine from a Spanish ancestor who, according to family gossip, was one of the founders of the town, back in the early seventeenth century."

"Wow, how interesting, Tía," I noted. "Dad told me part of what happened to my great-grandfather, Gustavo Viejo, but I thought it was a bit of a joke, you know how he is with his Colombian stories. He told me that Gustavo Viejo's life was like that of the protagonist in *No One Writes to the Colonel* by García Márquez, the first book he ever gave me, I think when I was twelve or thirteen years old. With what you told me, added to what little I knew, I now understand better. Poor old Gustavo Viejo, those years of waiting must have taken a toll on him. Now that you tell me that, I also remember that grandfather told me something about great-grandmother Solita because she inherited the hacienda where they went on vacation when he was a boy. Grandpa would tell me those stories in such detail that I imagined myself within them as if I were seeing everything through his eyes: the grassy backyard behind the old colonial house with balconies with iron railings, the hillside by which you reached the creek, the fruit trees and the bamboo-cane guaduales, and the sugar cane crops and the sugar mill and the unrefined sugarcane panela bricks that are so tasty, that he always used to say was good for your health."

"Now, that story is no longer mine," I remarked, feeling a knot in my stomach. "There's a lie that changes everything."

"You will always belong to that family, Francisco; your dad too. The lie doesn't erase the love with which I was there for your dad and you, and that you grew up with too. That love is unconditional and permanent. I will never stop loving you two and consider you my closest family. Never, cariño."

"Thank you Tía. I love you."

"Furthermore, having another family enriches you," Tía Astrid added. "It gives you multiple storylines and more nuances. And in some way –by extension, as you say– it's also my family, though remote and unknown. So, I'm going to Tocaima to investigate. I will stay at least a week; it's about time I give myself a much-needed holiday."

"You're going by yourself?"

"I'll ask Juana Medina if she wants to come with me. I suspect that my questions about your biological grandfather have to whet her appetite for research. She's fascinated by those kinds of stories and she knows how to do it properly."

SEVENTEEN

Altamira Fine Art occupied a warehouse next to a rickety, olive-green, five-story industrial building that looked abandoned. It was on a street I'd never walked on, though only a few yards from Thirty-Sixth Avenue where I used to jog on weekends, or walk on rainy days towards Roosevelt Island, to watch the Manhattan skyline, the promised land as Dad used to say back then. The warehouse had a metal rolling steel door covered in graffiti and, to one side, a regular door. The only indication that this was the place I was looking for was a small handwritten sign under the doorbell.

A skinny Asian man of medium height opened the regular door. He didn't say a word, just raised his eyebrows.

I asked him –in English– if I could speak to Mr. Cárdenas. The man looked at me curiously and shook his head no.

"Speak Spanish?"

"A little bit," he replied.

"Is Mr. Cárdenas there?"

"We are not open to the public," declared a man who arrived behind the Asian man in a loud voice. He had a vague Colombian accent.

"I urgently need to speak to Mr. Cárdenas," I said.

"There is no one by that name here."

"He is the owner of this business."

The man went out the door. He was stocky, but not as tall as me.

He looked me in the eye and blinked, a gesture of defiance. "What do you want?"

"I have an old piece of furniture that needs restoration," I said. It was the first thing that occurred to me.

"Who gave you this address?"

"I found it on the Internet," I said, and looked up and down the street. I had the feeling that someone was watching us.

"I don't know anything about that. Leave me your name and phone number; I will give your information to the manager."

"I don't have a pencil and paper," I lied.

The stocky man nodded at the Asian, and he turned around and went back in. From where I was standing, I could see that the warehouse was large and well-lit, where several men, at least five, were doing woodwork on a large workbench. I heard the noise of a table saw and pieces of lumber falling on the floor.

"Would you mind if I took a look?"

"I'm sorry, but this is private property," the man said, his face grimacing with impatience. "Also, I'm not authorized to let anyone in, he added."

The man was wearing a factory jumpsuit and work boots. He had a new mobile phone; mine was an older model of the same make. I also noticed that he was wearing an old silver crucifix around his neck, perhaps a family heirloom; Dad used to have pieces like that in the store.

"Are you Mexican?" I asked.

The man looked me in the eye with sudden hostility.

"Don't worry. I'm not from La Migra."

The Asian man returned and handed me a notebook and a pen.

I wrote down my first name and my mobile number.

The stocky man said, "Have a nice day," turned his back on me, and left. The skinny Asian man smiled; he was missing several teeth up front, and closed the door behind him.

I was certain that something of profound significance lurked within that warehouse, entwined with my past, my history, and my lineage. The graffiti on the metal roll-up door, proclaiming "MASTER YOUR HEART," struck me as a poignant warning. It dawned on me that I had encountered that phrase before, perhaps in another building or context. Back when a cryptic graffiti artist painted mysterious messages across the city. A panoramic closed-circuit television camera dangled from the ceiling in one corner of the facade, a vigilant eye overseeing the place. Someone was watching, safeguarding whatever secrets lay within. I retrieved my mobile from my backpack and took a photo of the graffiti; after that, I crossed the street and took a photo of the entire building.

I started to make my way back to Thirty-Sixth Avenue, but at some point, I told myself there was no point going home. I had to, at the very least, watch who came in and out of the warehouse. Although it was something I couldn't do, I realized; not at the moment. I needed a place from which I could watch without being seen, a car, for example, like in the movies. The presence of a toothless Asian man added an intriguing layer to the mystery. From his skin tone and the features of his face, I surmised that he was from Southeast Asia. Sachiko, my old Japanese girlfriend, had taught me to tell East Asians from Southeast Asians based on bearing, skin tone, and the shape of the eyes. Perhaps he was Vietnamese; it occurred to me that he looked like one of the waiters at the restaurant in Chinatown where we went with Natalia and Ricardo. Or southern Chinese, from Fujian, I had watched at school a documentary about the Fujianese diaspora scattered around the world. I thought of *A Chinese Story*, an Argentine film featuring Ricardo Darín, one of Dad's favorites. We had seen it three or four times. Dad identified with Darín's character, who owned a small hardware store in Buenos Aires, and, due to an absurd set of circumstances, ends up taking care of a Chinese immigrant who has just arrived in Argentina. He used to say that his life was like that of the ill-tempered hardware store owner, a statement not without merit, the two were owners of businesses in which they invested all their lives and did not produce the profit and satisfaction that they expected. When the character of Darín said in the movie, "Life is a great nonsense, an absurdity," Dad repeated the phrase, imitating an Argentine accent; it was something he enjoyed doing; I suppose he did it well, I can't tell an Argentine accent from a Peruvian one, even a Spanish one. Dad likes to say that I have no ear for non-Colombian accents. I told him once that he was just like him, cantankerous and morose, adjectives that he had taught me when I was little. To top it off, you look like him, I added. He replied: You're right about that, I am as handsome as he;

though taller, Darín is tiny. Dad sometimes would come up with childish nonsense.

I speculated that the toothless Asian at the warehouse had migrated to South America first and then to the United States. Perhaps he secured his visa because of mastery in some art or craft, and someone recruited him to work at Altamira Fine Art, a business harboring secrets and stories, which I would have to investigate.

I wanted to call Tía Astrid to share what I'd seen, but then I remembered that on Fridays, she had lunch with her friend Juana Medina, a rendezvous that consumed the entire afternoon. It crossed my mind that they could be more than just friends.

I turned around and decided to drop by my old neighborhood in Astoria; I hadn't done it since I moved to Manhattan. I remembered that there was a new Colombian restaurant near the Broadway subway station, touted as a must-stop on a foodie tour of Queens by the New York Times. I would call Ricardo and tell him I would buy him a beer and that I was starting my fieldwork.

That night Ana was going to a Broadway musical; her aunt had secured free tickets for her. She invited me to come along, but I declined, reminding her that I didn't like 1950s Americana.

EIGHTEEN

Ricardo and I had to wait for a table for almost half an hour at *Tierra Natal*, the Colombian restaurant on Broadway. The place was spacious, like an industrial warehouse, and open to the street, with some tables on the sidewalk. The decoration was peculiar and colorful. A great variety of objects hung from the ceiling: bicycles, horse saddles, spurs, bells, corn mills, ceramic cups, plates and vases, a hammock woven with tricolor threads like the Colombian flag, with a mannequin sleeping on it, and many other everyday objects. The atmosphere was festive, groups of family and friends occupied the tables, I assumed mostly Colombians, who chatted animatedly. In the background, above the conversations and laughter, the chords of traditional vallenato, a peasant song, guitars, and percussion could be heard.

"A Colombian spaceship," Ricardo commented. The hostess led us to our table in a corner. As soon as I sat down, I noticed a woman at the table next to ours beckoning to me. Squinting my eyes in the dimmed lights, I recognized Angela, my old high school friend. However, her attire was more formal than I remembered—a tight black dress with a round neckline, long sleeves, and high heels.

"Hello handsome, long time no see," she said in Spanish, something that sounded out of place, odd, dissonant. The

Angela I remembered never spoke Spanish to me. In my memory, she always spoke English with a heavy New York accent.

"Hi," I said and looked into her eyes. "I almost didn't recognize you."

"Have I changed so much?"

"You sound different, that's all." And, "you look gorgeous," I thought.

Angela got up and gave me a tight hug. It took me back to the last time we saw each other at her graduation party in Long Island.

"I missed you, you know," I whispered in her ear in English.

"Missed you too," she replied, also in English.

"Francisco, the person who helped me survive High School," she announced in Spanish to her friends –two young women about our age, and a man a little older, perhaps in his early forties.

I shook their hands. One of the young women, Paola, coughed a little, and looked surprised, as if we knew each other from before, though I was sure we didn't. The other, Yasmín, a brunette, said, in Spanish, "I'm at your service," an expression I hadn't heard in a long time. The older man, Javier, made a rather formal bow with his head that gave me the impression that he was some sort of business executive.

"My friend Ricardo; we go to school together," I said.

"Sit down with us and have a drink," Angela suggested. "Unless you're expecting company?"

Ricardo looked at me a little stunned.

"Sure," I said. "It's just the two of us."

Angela pointed to the free chairs, indicating with a smile that I sit next to her. "You have to bring me up to date with your life," she told me in English, in the confidential tone of hers I knew well.

As Ricardo sat down, Paola started to chat with him animatedly. Across the table, Yasmín said something to Javier in a whisper that made him put a hand to his ear to listen to her.

Angela said that she had found out about Dad's illness and that he had returned to Colombia. She added that she was sorry to hear that, and told me that her father was also ill, had recently been diagnosed with throat cancer, and was undergoing chemotherapy.

"It's really good to see you," she said after a pause and winked at me.

"And your husband?" I asked. Dad told me that he is from Jersey.

"My ex," Angela confessed with a sigh of irritation. "I got divorced last year and decided to come back to New York." I told her I was sorry and she reassured me that it was nothing, it hadn't been traumatic, far from it. "Give me the lowdown, I want to know what happened, I urged. Angela looked me in the eye half-pretending to be mad, as she used to do; it was her way to see whether I was serious or not.

"Will do, if you promise to do the same."

I shook my head yes.

"The first months were torture," she started. "I didn't understand anyone and no one understood me except my mom and my little sisters, though the little bitches would make fun of my mistakes. After a few weeks, I enrolled in Spanish as a Second Language program at a private university that changed my life. At the end of two semesters, one of my teachers helped me apply to a training program for instructors of Spanish as a Second Language. It wasn't easy, it took two years, but voilà: I became a Spanish teacher."

"Congrats," I said and raised my glass. From across the table Javier had served us shots of *aguardiente*.

"I got a job at a language school and things were looking up, I mean I had the money for my expenses: in Bogotá, there are a million things to do. I had a good time, I got along with my mom and my sisters and made a few friends. My romantic life was zero, zilch, though. I went out with several men my age, but I couldn't connect with any of them; truth be told, they all seemed cut from the same cloth: conventional and conservative like my dad. I met Manny, my ex, through a colleague who had been his teacher. He is of Italian descent; he'd spent several years in Colombia working in real estate investment and consulting, first with a company in New York and, later, with some Canadians with whom he entered into a business partnership. From the first moment, we got along very well; we understood each other perfectly. He was, is, ten years older than I, but he felt like someone of my generation, he reminded me of you, in fact: a bit formal, kind, and deep down a bit shy. After a few months, he proposed to me and I accepted. On our honeymoon we went to Italy, Rome, and Venice. We had a blast, Manny likes to travel five-star, he is very generous. On our return, we settled in a house in Chía, on the outskirts of Bogotá. All very hunky dory until then. After six or seven months, I found out that he was cheating on me with the same colleague who introduced him to me. She told me about it herself because she found out that he was dating other women too, some college students. Go figure! Frankly, I was surprised. I never would have guessed it. He was somewhat shy, in bed, I mean. I didn't care, nor that he traveled a lot, sometimes we hardly saw each other on weekends. To make a long story short, I asked him for a divorce, but he wasn't open to that. My mom suggested that we do a little sleuthing on him and we discovered that he was not only an inveterate Don Juan but that his consulting business was a kind of dating and marriage agency for American men who wanted to marry Colombian women. When I sent him a copy of the report from the detective agency, he agreed to the divorce. After a few months, I realized that my life was no longer in Colombia and here I am. I work as a teacher in a private school and I live with my dad. We finally made peace and now I like him, we are good friends.

"And you?" she asked and looked me in the eye.

"I'm still a bit formal, kind, and deep down shy," I said.

Angela put one hand on her mouth and with the other punched me on the arm. Ricardo and Paola, who were immersed in conversation, turned to look.

"Your little friend hasn't changed since high school," Angela said jokingly.

"You're telling me," Ricardo commented sarcastically, also in English, and raised his eyebrows.

Angela looked at me again and asked me if I was already married.

I shook my head.

"My dad told me that you go out with a yuppie Bogotá girl," Angela said and made a face of feigned surprise.

"Neither one nor the other," I countered. "You'll meet her someday if you behave." Then, in a low voice, I asked her if she was dating Javier.

"No, you're wrong as usual," Angela replied in a whisper. "He's a friend of my dad's, he's a journalist and a blogger and lives in Bangkok or Singapore, I get the two cities confused. He's leaving tomorrow, and we're here to celebrate. Yasmin and Paola are my friends; I met them in Bogotá. They also live far away, one in Tokyo, and the other in Dubai. They are staying with me for a few days; they both have green cards and have to set foot in the US every once in a while to keep their legal status."

"Speaking of Colombians," I interrupted. "I'm looking for a guy named Carlos Cárdenas. He owns Altamira Art, a fine furniture workshop in Long Island City. Do you know him?"

"Yeah sure, everyone in Astoria knows him, although he hasn't been in New York long, a couple of years, I think. If you hadn't gone yuppie and moved to Manhattan you would have already met him. He comes to this restaurant a lot, it's the new place to be. He is a bit eccentric: he dresses like an old-fashioned *cachaco* gentleman of yesteryear: bespoke double-breasted suits, and rabbit-felt fedoras. He lives in a big house near the Thirty-Six Avenue station, where he hosts a barbecue or a party every two or three months. He always invites the same people, usually business owners and people who do politics in the community."

"What do you want with him?" Angela asked and crossed her arms.

"I suspect that Cárdenas was the one who stole a bargueño from my dad," I said in a low voice. "Do you remember that I told you about it?"

At that moment the noise of china smashing against the floor was heard as well as somebody shouting something. Several people got up from their chairs, others turned to look. The music suddenly stopped.

"Nothing happened, calm down," said one of the waiters aloud. Those who stood up took their seats again and the chorus of animated voices returned.

"Do you think it was Carlos Cárdenas?" Angela whispered.

"Almost one hundred per cent sure."

"He just left the restaurant."

"The tall man with a long face and hooked nose who wore a Greek cap? He had caught my attention when he came in, talking with an attractive young brunette."

"Yes, but don't go running after him, people know him in this area."

"It wouldn't have occurred to me to follow him," I said. "It's enough that I know where to find him. I'll find a way to talk to him."

NINETEEN

The next morning I received a call from a private number. I was going to ignore it, but I got a hunch and answered.

"This is Carlos Cárdenas speaking. My employees tell me that you came to look for me at the factory. How can I help you?" he asked, his tone neutral and measured, with just a trace of a *cachaco* Bogotá accent, like Dad's.

"I have a colonial piece of furniture that is a bit damaged," I said. "I'm told you're a restorer."

"What kind of furniture?"

"A Spanish colonial bargueño from the 16th century."

"In that case, I can't help you," he said after a pause in which I thought I heard a metallic sound, I assumed he was in the warehouse.

"Why not?"

"I see that you're not well-informed. If it is a genuine 16th-century antique, it is better to seek the advice of an expert. If you like, I can give you the name of someone in Manhattan, perhaps the only person who could help you. Where do you live?"

"On the Upper West Side," I lied.

"It's an antique dealer in the West Village," he said. I trust him completely, you can tell him I sent you. His name is Windsor, just that. Mister Windsor. He is the owner of Goldfinch Antiques, down on MacDougal. Anything else?"

I told him no and that if I had another question I would call him back.

"As you wish," he said, rather dryly, and hung up.

"I didn't know you lived on the Upper West Side," Ana said as she left our bedroom. She was getting dressed when the phone rang.

I explained to her what it was about. "I didn't want to give him any specific information," I clarified.

"You don't want him to see your hand?" Ana asked and sat next to me. In the distance, menacing clouds loomed over the East River.

"I don't want him to know who I am yet," I replied.

"Same difference."

"I don't know how he would react."

"Do you want to unmask him as your aunt Astrid says happened to him in Bogotá?"

"I have no evidence that he is doing the same in New York," I said. "Also, it does not concern me. I'm not the guardian of taracea orthodoxy. What interests me about him is knowing why he stole the bargueño from Dad. Being a pirate restorer, he could just make another."

"Unless there's something special about that one."

"Yes, I've also thought that," I said and went over to the bargueño, next to the bookcase. I took out one of the drawers and looked at it from all sides. It occurred to me that perhaps there was a signature or a special mark on the wooden surface, but I didn't see anything out of the ordinary. I did the same with the other five with the same result. When placing them again, two of them did not fit well. I reversed the order in which I put them and realized that I was wrong the first time.

"There is a key in the animal engravings," I said.

"Do you know from which bestiary they come?"

"Not yet," I admitted, taking out the drawers again and attempting to place each of them in a different spot. None of them fit.

"There's only one way to read it."

"You talk to me in riddles," Ana pointed out.

"The owl can only be on the top to the right. Below is the elephant; at the bottom, the lion; in the other row, the Griffin; the wolf in the middle, and the antelope, underneath. The question is: what is the reading order? From right to left? The other way around? Top to bottom or bottom to top? Maybe there is no narrative," I said somewhat annoyed.

"Of course, there is. You said it yourself that each drawer goes in a certain place."

"The key to the reading must be in the illuminated bestiary that Rosiñol del Valle stole," I concluded.

The next day I called Tía Astrid first thing in the morning and told her about my adventures in Astoria.

"I can't believe it," she said, and then she repeated it with more emphasis. Then she asked, in a tone of concern: "What are you going to do?"

"Nothing, Tía," I replied. "There is nothing I can do. But I want to talk to him; I'd like to hear his story. I doubt he wants to do it, but I'm going to ask him anyway. On the other hand, I sent another email to Sara Ruiz with this new information. I think it would be convenient for her to meet Rosiñol del Valle, now known as Carlos Cárdenas, pirate restorer, and polyglot adventurer. But she hasn't replied to my email."

"Patience, Francisco. Did you write to your other cousin, the one in Dubai?"

"Yes. Also no answer."

Tía Astrid grunted.

"Do you remember if Dad had a disagreement with the owner of the Goldfinch store on MacDougal Street when you were living with us? I have a childhood memory of Dad complaining about the Manhattan antique dealers."

"I don't remember cariño," she replied. "Those were difficult years for him, you know that. Gustavo thought that the New York antiques community would welcome him with open arms, or at least that they would treat him as equals. But now that you mention it," she said with some emphasis after a short silence, "I remember I went with him to an antique shop in the West Village, but I don't know if it was on MacDougal; for some reason, I think it was close to that famous intersection, the one in Kubrick's *Eyes Wide Shut*. It was a large place, in the basement of an apartment building. The owner was a tall, paunchy man who spoke with a European accent. Gustavo had left him on consignment a beautiful taracea jewelry box from the 1930s with bone and tortoiseshell inlays, but the antique dealer sold it for a much lower price than they had agreed to. For Gustavo, more than a business matter, it was a matter of culture. 'In this city nobody knows a damn about Spanish heritage,' I remember him saying. Why do you ask?"

"I'll tell you later, for now, I'm just connecting the dots."

"How is Angelita?" Tía Astrid asked. "How did she seem to you? I know that she got married and divorced. In Bogotá, we spoke a couple of times, but we never saw each other. I invited her several times to the apartment for drinks, but she was always busy with one thing and the other. She invited me to the wedding, but I was in Santa Marta on holiday. To be honest, Angelita and I are from parallel universes."

"I don't understand."

"Because you are dense."

"And you are denser than a neutron star," I said, as Dad would have.

Tía Astrid laughed. "I'm glad Angelita got divorced," she added in a relieved tone. When she told me about the guy, I suspected he was up to no good. I didn't imagine anything about the business side of things, but I said to myself: 'He is one of those men who come to this country looking for an exotic and submissive little woman.'"

"If it makes them happy, I don't see anything wrong with it."

"Whatever, Francisco."

"Tía, can I ask you something personal?"

"Why am I not married?"

"Why didn't things work out with D'Artagnan?"

"For a thousand reasons, cariño. I already told you that Emilio changed in New York, I suppose I did too, but not so much. In Bogotá, we got along famously. But after a few months in New York, he was already very comfortable in the city, he made friends easily, spent time in Manhattan with them, and became conceited. One fine day he said: 'New York is too small for me, I'm going to see the world.' He got married and went to Europe. And now after a Parisian period worthy of a novel he returns triumphantly with the name of a musketeer."

"Why are you in a bad mood with him?"

"Excuse me, Francisco." You know that the subject irritates me.

"Why don't you come to New York for a few weeks this summer, Tía? A friend of mine asked me to house-sit for the whole month of July in Kingston, on the Hudson. That way you can meet. By then I won't have exams or anything. What do you say?

TWENTY

Ana's Tía Margarita was a woman in her sixties, with wavy dyed blond hair that fell to her shoulders. She was very friendly, though somehow theatrical; her gestures seemed well calculated as if she had rehearsed them beforehand. I couldn't help but think of female characters her age in Almodóvar's films.

Her children, Jacobo and Alejandra, on the other hand, seemed very natural and friendly to me; like Ana. They both looked like twins, with long oval faces, dark eyes and hair, and full lips. I imagined that they inherited these features from their father; Tía Margarita had a round face and blue eyes.

The apartment was spacious – I had never seen one so large – with high ceilings and large windows overlooking Seventy-Second Street, almost on the corner of Central Park West. The decor was a mix of styles: modern living room furniture of Scandinavian design covered in neutral colored fabrics, a dining table made of thick rustic wood, abstract paintings, and black and white photographs covering the entirety of one of the walls, and numerous works of art on side tables such as African wooden statuettes, hand-painted ceramic vases with oriental motifs, and metal and wood marquetry boxes, among others. Built into two of the walls were bookshelves stocked with academic and art books, from what I could see.

As perhaps it was planned, the first topic of conversation was my fieldwork; Ana had told them that my research proposal had been approved. I explained the best way I could what I had in mind. Tía Margarita said: "How interesting that it is about the Colombian community." Her tone made me think that her family was not part of it, as if it were a different and distant ethnic group; although perhaps my reading was not objective, given the circumstances. Fortunately, at that moment a Colombian maid arrived –I could tell from her accent– with tea and an assortment of pastries. While she was serving us, I noticed that on a small table, there was a small chest coffer inlaid with various materials and drawings of hunting scenes that reminded me of the engravings in my bargueño.

"It's a Persian jewelry box, though some experts say that it could be Ottoman," Alejandra noted; she was sitting kitty-corner from me.

"An antique?" I asked.

"From the 19th century," she replied.

"A gift from Mehrdad," Alejandra's fiancé, Tía Margarita commented. "An heirloom of his family."

"My boyfriend is Persian," Alejandra offered.

"Mehrdad is from a very distinguished family," Tía Margarita hastened to add. "His parents fled Iran with the revolution and settled in Geneva, where he was born."

"An NYU political scientist," Ana added, and I remembered that she had once told me that he and her cousin had been dating since they were in high school. Also, it had not been easy because Tía Margarita had not agreed with the relationship due to the difference in religion, but that little by little she made peace with it over time.

"He is a visiting professor at the University of Macao," Jacobo said, and looked at his mobile, as if the information had come from there. "He was lucky; he was offered the job as soon as he graduated last year."

"Are you going to apply to that university?" Ana asked and Alejandra replied, "No." "It's a great place to travel but I don't see myself living there," she explained.

"You could research colonial architecture in Macau, cousin."

"Alejandra wrote her dissertation about Portuguese colonial art in Brazil," Tía Margarita explained, with some emphasis.

"The truth is that I would rather stay in New York. Mehrdad just applied for a position at Columbia and I have the option of taking an executive position with Christie's in a couple of years."

"She has just been promoted to curator of Latin American art," Tía Margarita noted, again with some emphasis.

"Terrific, cousin, I didn't know," said Ana and offered her a smile.

I also congratulated her, but in the interim, in the exchange of glances, I had the impression that there was something tense and unresolved between the two cousins. Ana had told me that of all her cousins in Colombia, five or six, Alejandra was the most competitive; she always wanted to be the best in everything, study at the best universities, get the best job, marry the ideal man, and things like that.

"How's your project going?" Alejandra asked Ana, in a tone that seemed somewhat feigned to me.

"Smooth sailing," Ana replied. "I'll start working on my dissertation proposal soon. Meanwhile, I am working with Professor Vartatian on a project related to the peace process in Colombia."

"Congrats cousin," said Alejandra, and like an echo the voices of Jacobo and Aunt Margarita joined in, without a trace of malice.

"Francisco inherited a colonial bargueño that contains a secret," Ana said, which surprised me as much as annoyed me. It was unexpected.

"Do you have any photos of it?" Alejandra asked.

I opened my mobile's photo app and showed her the pictures. Then and there, I remembered the moment when Rodrigues had asked me the very same question.

While Alejandra was examining the photo, I looked towards Central Park: I had never seen it from that perspective, we were on the fifteenth floor. In the distance, a cluster of tall and elongated clouds were sailing to the horizon.

"Do you know who the man in the engraving is?" Alejandra asked, her gaze still fixed on one of the pictures.

"I don't know," I replied. "My dad says that he was probably an Andalusian sage, although he didn't know exactly who or from what century. Professor Rodrigues at Fordham thinks it could be the prophet Noah from a XVI Mughal miniature painting."

"In that case, we look at the animal engravings," Alejandra remarked. "By chance, Dad has a medieval bestiary, a printed copy, of course, that can help us," she said and went to the bookcase behind her. "The owl on the top right could be read, depending on the context, as an anti-Semitic statement or slogan,"she said after a brief pause. "It's a nocturnal bird of prey, associated with evil, or with the devil. The small engravings on each of the four sides of the plate represent Christian birds preparing to fight the owl. The owl represents the antithesis of Christianity: Judaism."

"Evidence of what I've been saying," Jacobo, commented, in a tone loaded with irony. I was surprised that he was following the thread of the conversation; he'd been looking at his mobile for a while now.

"You see anti-Semitism everywhere, Jaques," Alejandra said in a tone of reproach.

"Please, children," Tía Margarita interrupted, a feigned smile on her face. "Let's not start with this boring topic, especially when we have company."

Alejandra winked at her brother, who was sitting on the sofa, in front of her, next to his mother. Ana, sitting to my right, looked for something in her bag, perhaps her mobile phone; it was something she did when she was nervous.

"What about the other animals?" I asked.

"The elephant represents the law or Jesus Christ, it depends on the context; the lion, nobility, and strength; the griffin is the guardian of justice; the wolf is associated with evil; the antelope depends, it can be the old and the new testament; I only know that the deer is the dragon's enemy. I'm going to check it out and I'll let you know, okay?"

"Sure," I said, and nodded, and in that instant, I had a sense of déjà vu, as if I had already lived through that moment. There was something about the present scene that was familiar to me. I looked at Alejandra who was still examining the photos, and it occurred to me that I'd seen her before. After a few moments, I remembered an actress from a Colombian series that we used to watch with Mom when we had just arrived in New York. She looked like her: her straight dark, and shiny hair down to her shoulders, her big, brown, almond-shaped eyes. In the television series, she played an antagonistic role, a wicked rich girl, with whom I was hopelessly in love; she took my breath away; she was perhaps the first woman I ever desired. An instant later, I realized Ana was looking at me intently.

"I'd like to see it in person," Alejandra said and she arched her eyes, perhaps a way of asking me when.

"I'll let you know," I said.

TWENTY ONE

Ana was quick to reproach me.

"I saw how you looked at Alejandra, don't think I'm blind," she said, her tone full of sarcasm, when we got home.

"I was looking at a memory," I ventured.

"Only you believe that. Do you mean that she reminds you of someone else from your past?"

"Something like that," I said. "It's complicated."

"This is what you always say to avoid calling things by their name," she said and took her jacket off. "Be completely honest," she snapped. "You like Alejandra. You flirted with her. Admit it."

"Alejandra reminds me of a girl I was in love with when I was ten years old," I said. "But she's not my type anymore."

"Classic line."

"I'm serious."

Ana changed her demeanor, and she half smiled at me. I realized in that instant that she was a bit theatrical, like her aunt, but better at it.

"Sometimes I hate my cousin."

"Because you compete with her."

"Because she's always had everything handed to her on a silver platter."

"I get it. That's what I told myself when we got to your Aunt Margarita's apartment." Despite myself, to my mind came the face of that woman, her chiseled face and blue eyes, so different from her children.

"What I don't understand is what Jacobo said."

"What he was going to say," you mean. "My aunt stopped him cold. It is a bone of contention in the family. It's not going to seem like a big deal, I'm sure, but you don't know how things are in Colombia."

"Quite different," I said.

"You hit it on the head, pirate. It is about the horrible possibility that an ancestor of the family was a crypto-Jew, a secret Jew. In an ultra-Catholic and patriotic family like ours it would be a great shame. Jacobo was the one who instigated everything, he was our grandmother's Valenzuela's favorite. She told him the secret story of her grandmother: her family was Jewish, and they had changed their names to come to the New World in the 16th century. But no one in the family believed it. It's just gossip, they would say. Jacobo then proposed that to clear things up they should do DNA tests. Except for one of my aunts, we all agreed. Grandma's results were not conclusive: she had just twenty percent Ashkenazi Jewish DNA. Her children, including my Mom, had roughly half of that, and the grandchildren, me included between five and eight percent. There is no way of knowing the percentage of either of my great-grandparents, so we concluded that such ancestors were over four generations in the past, and probably only one of them, not both, so the ties are very weak. On balance, the old gossip had a grain of truth that might have meant something in the past but not at all now."

"The story has ingredients for a novel," I said. "An inheritance would have to be added to intrigue. And then adapt it for the silver screen."

"Right you are again," Ana said. "That's the underlying theme of the novel that Jacobo is writing. He didn't have to go far into the issue of inheritance. My aunt Margarita's grandfather was taken off the will because he belonged to the political party opposite to which all the other men in the family belonged."

"My grandfather Gustavo used to tell me stories like that. Has he finished writing it?"

"He says he's halfway through."

"Is he writing it in Spanish?"

"No, he is writing it in French."

"I'm jealous," I admitted.

"You shouldn't be," Ana said, and looked me in the eye.

"Another thing that caught my attention was the paintings and photos in the living room," I commented and kissed her on the forehead. "You kept looking at them."

"Interesting that you noticed that. The paintings are very expressive and atmospheric, they look like volcanic eruptions," she said. "They are by a Californian painter that Alejandra knows and admires. She recently told me that it was the kind of painting she would've done had she gone to art school. She always wanted to be a painter, you know? When we were little, we played career fairs, she always chose visual arts, sometimes she was a painter, others a sculptor, or draftswoman, and so on. It was no surprise, Tía Margarita majored in fine arts at university. Although she never did anything with it. She married an endocrinologist, became a homemaker and left her art for the weekends. She had her studio in the back of their house, and sometimes we would play there. One day, my aunt showed us how to paint with oils. Then she bought each of us an easel. She wasted her money on me, I just doodled. But Alejandra was a natural. Since then, I think she dreamed of becoming a painter. But when she graduated from high school in Geneva and said that she wanted to study painting, my aunt Margarita convinced her to study art history first."

"What a privileged life," I said and thought of Alejandra, which in my mind transformed itself into the likeness of that actress from that Colombian series that Mom and I watched so many years ago. For some reason, I remembered a scene in which the evil character I was so fond of wakes up one morning and looks at herself in the mirror admiring her brown eyes or perhaps just looking at them, I don't know, but I couldn't take my eyes off that scene. We watched the series on DVDs, and I would rewind it over and over again just to look at her eyes. With that image still in my mind, I looked at Ana and desired her. But I would have to wait still.

"And the black and white photographs?" I asked.

"Those are Uncle Guillermo's," Ana replied, and threw herself on the sofa, as she sometimes did in bed, with a playful jump. "Photography has always been his hobby," she added. "I understand he took classes at The New School. Amongst them are photos of the family across three generations. The entire wall is a kind of album, which he rearranges every week, like some sort of curatorial practice."

"Are you in any of those photos?"

"There is one in which I'm with Alejandra. It's a beautiful photo, we are holding hands, her hair is in braids, mine is messy and wild, at my grandparents' finca in Tolima, near Ibagué. I miss that place you know. There, I learned so many things, to ride a horse, to fish with my grandfather, to climb trees, to talk to animals. The three of us, Alejandra, Jacobo and I were inseparable. We spent Christmas there, you don't know what that was like, what sweetness of life. Of course, there were dangers, my grandparents had armed guards around the property; our peace of mind had that price."

"You had a privileged life in Colombia."

"Only when I was with my grandparents or with Tía Margarita, dear pirate. I have already told you that my mother is the black sheep of the family. She married my dad who wasn't, isn't, to use gringo terms, white, like them. He was not a lawyer or a doctor, but a small businessman, owner of a spare parts factory, living in a strictly middle-class and diverse neighborhood, a little bit of everything, not far from the National University, Dad's Alma Mater, in a different world than Tía Margarita and my grandparents."

"I'm not in the mood for another of your social justice in Colombia monologues, so I'm going to turn the lights off," I said. Ana countered, "Ah well, okay, let's play hide and seek." In the semi-darkness, I saw her beckoning with her finger to come closer.

"It's about time," I said.

TWENTY-TWO

I found myself in a lucid dream, a story that I vaguely remembered from somewhere, perhaps within a dream itself. It was cold. I stood in a small square dominated by an equestrian statue. To one side, a German brewery pub stood, where, in times long past, I'd shared dinner with a tall and exotic woman whose face eluded my memory. It wasn't clear if this was my own experience, a figment of a dream, or a fragment read in a novel. On the opposite side stood a towering building, clouds streaking overhead, a pale moon hiding behind them. It was where I lived, I remembered. Somehow, I got to the apartment and I was taken aback: someone was looking out the window of the living room overlooking the square. A clock read three in the morning. Then, abruptly, I woke up—sweating, heart racing.

Ana was not in bed. I recalled her mentioning a meeting with Vartatian and Marta Salazar. She said it as if to herself before saying goodnight after our fiery bedroom game. I felt a bit weird, uncomfortable in my own skin, perhaps I had not slept enough. I went to the kitchen and opened Ana's laptop; I had forgotten to charge the battery of mine. Arvo Pärt's *Silentium* played in the music app; Ana had been listening to it with her headphones. It was paused, almost at the end. She had insomnia, I concluded. Lately, she wasn't sleeping well, school worried her too much. The one thing that soothed her was listening to music by the Estonian composer, whose music, she said, was made from the raw material of her dreams, and her tears. I pictured her sitting on the sofa watching the East River go out to sea, her hair down, her feet bare.

In my mailbox I found a message from Ana, a question: See you at the Japanese restaurant at seven? I replied: "Yes, of course, and good luck with your meeting."

I opened the map app and located the Japanese restaurant, Natsuko; then the Goldfinch –a velvety word– the antique store and D'Artagnan's bar. They stood at a short distance from each other, each beckoning in a different direction, forming an isosceles triangle. Were I to add Altamira Fine Art, the pirate restorer's factory across the East River, it would complete an arrow pointing southwest.

Looking at the river from the open kitchen I repeated the word Natsuko. I'd looked up its meaning on Wikipedia. It was something like attachment, a kind of affection, Dad had explained it to me before, many years ago; as a child, I was always asking about the meaning of everything. I closed my eyes and saw myself with Dad at the Natsuko when we used to go to dinner together on Fridays after my classes. We almost always ordered the same thing, an obento with salmon or chicken, sashimi raw fish, and sushi rolls. Dad got along with her. No, it was more than that: he liked the owner, Noriko-san, a woman his age, slender and elegant. He'd known her from the time he and Mom used to have dinner there; I would stay at home with Tía Astrid, I remembered we would play cards or checkers. Now that I thought about it, Dad never stopped going there. Sometimes he would come home late and he would say, I had something to do in the Village and I ate at the Natsuko, it was delicious, we have to go back soon. The last time we went, almost two years ago, as we left I asked him: "Dad, do you like Noriko-san?" He replied: "Of course I like her, how could I not, she's a remarkable woman," as if it were a joke; as if saying: "What makes you think that?" But it could be the other way around. Maybe he was in love with her. Maybe the two of them were in love with each other. Are they? Were they? I wondered. It had just occurred to me. Why didn't I think about it before? I felt somewhat guilty. I didn't know anything about Dad's love life. I just didn't conceive of it. I always thought he didn't remarry as a way of being loyal to her memory.

"Long time no see," Noriko-san greeted me at the door of Natsuko. This caught me by surprise, although there was nothing strange about her remembering me. She asked me if Dad was coming, and I said, "not this time." I was going to tell her that he was in Colombia, but it occurred to me that it would lead to more questions I didn't want to be asked and I decided to shut up. Noriko-san looked me straight in the eye and then gave me a bow that seemed overly formal.

Ana, Natalia, and Ricardo were chatting animatedly when I joined the table. It was the best in the house, by the only window. A black stretch limousine with tinted windows passed by on the street, and one of the passengers opened the window a crack to dispose of a cigarette butt.

"Good news," Ana announced after our greetings. "I'm going to teach a class at Lang College next semester and I am free to choose the subject."

"Congrats," I said, giving her another hug. Natalia and Ricardo said, well done Ana, you deserve it, and they toasted. Ana then shared details of her meeting with Vartatian and Marta Salazar. They were going to be co-chairs of her dissertation committee and suggested she teach a class on either the anthropology of museums or anthropology of art. The syllabus would help define her research topic and write her proposal.

Natalia asked Ana if she was still considering the Colombian Caribbean for her fieldwork, and she replied that of course, it was the only thing that was non-negotiable. Natalia and Ricardo said they would visit her, they were planning a trip to Cartagena the following summer.

"Of course, it will be a pleasure," Ana replied, placing her hand on mine.

For me, it would be the first time; I don't know the Colombian Caribbean, I admitted. For some reason, I noticed that the limousine that had passed by earlier was now parked on the other side of the street. Perhaps its passengers were dining in one of the nearby restaurants, though not in the Natsuko –no one had come in since I arrived.

"To the four of us, in Cartagena, next summer," Ana declared, raising her glass.

Noriko-san served us dinner, a gesture reserved for her favorite customers, as Dad had told me. As she retreated behind the counter, a trace of sadness lingered on her face, although it could have been something else. I couldn't be objective that night.

How did it go with Goldfinch? Ana asked. Ricardo and Natalia are up to date with your inquiries.

"I went there after lunch," I explained. "Mr. Windsor, the owner is quite a character. He is not American or British but Dutch. He told me: 'Yes, of course I remember your father, I still have some items that I bought from him for my collection.' He then went to his office and brought a medium-size taracea frame with bone and tortoiseshell marquetry and carved rippled molding, like the one on the edge of my bargueño drawers, but thicker. Then he invited me to have a coffee and told me about the development of techniques for making Dutch rippled mouldings, a topic that dovetailed into a lecture on the history of Renaissance decorative arts. He is a very nice man, and I didn't want to interrupt him, but he took his time. He explained that he was an amateur historian. When I asked about Spanish or Latin American colonial bargueños, he replied that he had recently acquired one from Colombia that he had restored –it was in great disrepair–and it was currently being appraised at Christie's. I smiled to myself and wondered how much Vartatian had gotten for it. After that, he asked me how Dad was doing; the rumor had reached him of his early illness. I told him the truth, and I felt at ease with him. Besides, he somehow reminded me of my grandfather Gustavo, with his old-fashioned gentlemanly manners.

"Did he know Carlos Cárdenas or Rosiñol del Valle?" Ana inquired.

"He told me the names didn't ring a bell, though he admitted that he had a terrible memory of foreign names. At that moment some clients arrived and he told me to come see him again when I had time and was in the neighborhood. I told him that I would gladly do it and that I'd enjoyed talking to him.

"At least you learned something," Ricardo remarked.

"I'll go back in a couple of weeks," I said. "I would like to know what's in the report from Christie's. At that moment the limousine that was parked in front drove off and I realized that across the street was the costume shop in the basement of the building where Tía Astrid thought the antique store was. She must have dined at the Natsuko at some point, either with Dad or by herself during one of her brief trips to New York, and the opposite side of the street had triggered memories of *Eyes Wide Shut*. Yet, it wasn't the same street as in the film. Dad, always the inveterate movie buff, had once informed me that Kubrick filmed all the Greenwich Village street scenes in London.

TWENTY-THREE

As I left a meeting at the university's Financial Aid Office –one more reminder of my absolute dependence on student loans and the uncertain future looming if I failed to secure a tenure-track job the next academic year–I noticed a voicemail from Tía Astrid. It was probably a response to the message I left her the night before. When she didn't answer the phone, I figured that she had gone out to dinner with Juana Medina; they were in Tocaima where they were to meet with my second cousin's family. The fleeting idea crossed my mind that she and Juana were lovers.

"Yesterday, I met Adriana, your second cousin," Tía Astrid began with her tone of enthusiasm. "She unexpectedly flew to Colombia from Dubai to sign legal documents and renew her passport. You'd like her; she is nice, uncomplicated, and talks a mile a minute! She reminds me a bit of Angelita, she has that air of independence and fearlessness. She asked me to tell you that she got your email and will soon write back; she's been quite busy with travel and family matters. Guess what? She also knows who Mr. Windsor is! She told me that he has clients in Dubai. She met him through a lawyer friend of hers with contacts in the international art and antique market. It seems there are many nouveau riche in Dubai eager to acquire works of art to show the world their cosmopolitan streak. But the real kicker, Francisco: Windsor has a partner, a Spanish antique restorer in New York, who travels frequently to Dubai. She doesn't know him yet, but she will soon. That guy must be Rosiñol del Valle, aka Carlos Cárdenas. It has to be; too many coincidences, she added with some emphasis.

They invited me over for tea, by the way, she went on after a short pause. I tell you now so next time we talk I can tell you a couple of things that I've been thinking about. In any case, Don Aldemar is a prince: humble, well-mannered, and helpful, one of those people who immediately inspire confidence. Affectionate too, you don't know how he looks at his daughter and how he talks to Graciela, his wife. Graciela is like Adriana in spirit, but a little clueless. They are a very beautiful family, very loving. Like us, if I say so myself. You're lucky Francisco. They live on the outskirts of town, next to the old royal cobbled stone road. It's an old house, colonial style, with decor from a hundred years ago; a gold mine for an antique dealer: the rustic wood furniture, the hand-painted crockery, everything. At least a dozen taracea frames with tortoiseshell inlays and engraved bone plates hung on the walls. And the bargueño, of course, which is the original XVI century *Arca de Noé* bargueño. The real deal! Adriana told me that the *Arca de Noé* in *Museo del Virreinato* is a twin made more or less at the same time, but with a Christian motif, the engraving in the central plate is of St. Francis of Assisi, patron saint of animals. I'll send you photos of all of us and the bargueño in a few minutes. I have to go now, cariño. Let's try to connect. A little kiss.

At home, I opened the photos on my laptop. There were six. In the first one, from left to right, was Tía Astrid wearing a blue linen dress that always makes her look ten years younger. Next to her, was Juana Medina, in jeans and a T-shirt, beautiful and enigmatic, as I remembered her. In the middle was the young woman who would be my cousin Adriana, who indeed looked like Angela from a distance, round face, lively eyes, and light brown hair. I imagined greeting her. I said in a low voice, hi Adriana. The woman next to her would be her mother, Graciela, who is an older version of Adriana, though shorter and with salt and pepper hair. To the far right stood my great-uncle Aldemar, a tall slender man, his posture slightly stooped, perhaps on purpose, so as not to emphasize his height.

The other photos were of the taracea frames and the bargueño. Because the frames were hung on several walls, I could figure out the layout of the house, the bedrooms around the living and dining room, and a kitchen in the back with nineteen-sixties appliances. Looking at the pictures of the bargueño, I remembered what Professor Rodrigues said about the artist's signature and enlarged the images as much as possible. I took my laptop to the bargueño next to the bookshelf and compared the traces of the engravings. The drawers with animal ones looked the same and were positioned in the same order. The traces on the engraving of the bearded man wearing a turban on the central plate also looked pretty much the same. Still, I wasn't convinced.

"I needed to find the certificate of authenticity of my bargueño," I thought. Tía Astrid had told me that attached to it was a paper discussing its origins. I rummaged through the contents of the cardboard box that Dad had forgotten to go through before he went back to Colombia. If I remember correctly, Dad himself had told me he had put the certificate there.

It didn't take me long to find it. It was in a manila envelope along with other documents. The envelope bore a label that read, 2005 Accounts, which is why I had not examined its contents before. There were two pages printed on letterhead stationery from *Antigüedades Maya*, Grandpa Gustavo's antique store in Bogotá, dated March 1981, two years before I was born. The first was a detailed description of the bargueño and a color picture of it. The next page was a narrative certifying that an analysis of the materials and surfaces suggested that the wood used was from the latter part of the nineteenth century, and the marquetry inlays from the nineteen thirties or forties. It was therefore authenticated to be an antique from the first four decades of the twentieth century.

To my surprise, the certificate was written by Mom; it had her name, Miranda Velázquez, and her signature underneath, as well as her title, Antiques Licensed Expert, registered with the Bogotá Chamber of Commerce! It was a document that I had never seen before; surely it was always kept somewhere out of sight. After all, it was a reminder of the scam that somehow precipitated our trip to New York and changed our lives. It had been a long time since I had seen

Mom's name written down and her expressive signature: the M like a kind of rope or whip in the air, mid-flight, the cursive and crowded letters, which together gave it an elegant symmetry.

As a child, I was fascinated by my mother signing checks; she was in charge of bookkeeping at the store in Bogotá. She would hold the checkbook to her left and carefully place the fountain pen on the check –she never used a ballpoint pen– and sign in one quick burst. As she let the ink dry she would look at the ledger, perhaps to memorize the amount she would have to write on the next check. Once, while Mom and Dad were shopping and my grandmother Francisca was taking a nap, I went to Mom's desk, took out the checkbook, and tried to sign her name several times with the fountain pen –a feat that earned me a scolding from my grandmother Francisca and the laughter of Mom and Dad when they came back and discovered my failed attempt at forgery. I closed my eyes and saw it all over again; it's one of the memories that I used to evoke in my mind years ago, but less often now; that past is more distant every day.

Stapled with the certificate of authenticity was an academic paper titled, *Historia de la Taracea en Colombia* by Gustavo Reyes and Miranda Velázquez. It was typewritten, perhaps in the Olivetti that Mom and Dad had. I quickly checked; it was one of the things at home that we didn't want to sell when Dad decided to go back to Colombia. Ana, for some reason, decided that it didn't go with our furniture and put it away in the closet. In Astoria, we always had it on a bookcase shelf as decor.

The paper had six pages of text and two illustrations with three photos. The first part was about the origins of taracea in Syria and then in Al-Andalus, in medieval Iberia; the next was about its arrival in the New World; and the last, a close look at two pieces restored by a taracea master in Bogotá in the nineteen-sixties. I read this last section carefully. The first piece was the *Arca de Noé* bargueño made by a master craftsman in Santa Fe de Bogotá in 1780. It was commissioned by a distinguished official of the crown, Don Manuel Valenzuela de Cisneros. It was to stand next to an *estrado doméstico*, a wooden platform of Muslim Iberian origin, covered with rugs, cushions, and pillows, where his wife, Doña Francisca, entertained her friends.

The following paragraphs were a genealogy of Don Manuel's starting with his grandfather, a native of Seville, who traveled to the New World in 1774. I read diagonally the following paragraphs, made of names and dates until I found my maternal great-grandmother, Soledad Herrera, who was a relative of one of the descendants of Don Manuel's second wife, a man named Nicolás Ruiz Herrera. What was intriguing was that, according to the document, Nicolas Ruiz Herrera bequeathed the *Arca de Noé* bargueño, notable for its engravings of animals on bone plates, to the Museo del Virreinato in Bogotá, in 1942. How was it possible then that my great-grandmother Soledad Herrera had it in her possession so that she could bequeath it to my grandfather Gustavo?

The first of the three photos was of the *Arca de Noé* bargueño, the original from which I have a copy. I looked closely at the central engraving of the bearded man in a turban, there was something about the lines that seemed different to me. The next was of a taracea display table with engraved bone plates of floral motifs, a frosted glass top and sides, and slim legs with vertical tortoiseshell veneers. I had never seen it before, although Dad or Grandfather Gustavo might have had it at the store in Bogotá; they had several taracea tables, as far as I can recall. The last photo took up an entire page. The last photo took up a whole page. It was black and white and had an air of yesteryear, perhaps from the nineteen fifties. Three young women and an older man were standing looking through an empty taracea frame, as if it were a mirror. Underneath it was the taracea display table with the long legs of the previous picture, which suggested the man in the picture was the taracea master, and the young women, his three daughters. You couldn't see much of the older man, who was wearing a suit and a tie; the top portion of the frame crossed out the features of his face, only his bald head and broad forehead were visible.

There was a caption underneath: Taracea master Rafael Ruiz Gutiérrez and three of his daughters. Bingo! I exclaimed, and wondered about the mechanism of the universe: everything seemed to be connected in mysterious and unexpected ways.

TWENTY-FOUR

Tía Astrid called around midnight. I was working on an essay about my dissertation project for a university grant.

"We had a little emergency, but Gustavo is fine, cariño," she said without preamble. "Sometimes he behaves like a spoiled child. Do you know what he asked me? Why didn't I bring him some *achira* biscuits? He threw a tantrum this afternoon because they did not give him those biscuits he likes so much for dessert. One of the nurses went to the corner store and bought him a package, but he said – surprise, surprise – that he didn't like that brand, that they had to be of the brand he liked."

I shook my head and to my mind came the image of Dad savoring some achiras; he got them from a Colombian bakery in Jackson Heights. "Manna from heaven," he would say before putting one in his mouth. After tasting it, he would hum, um, ummm, how can something be ever so tasty?"

"Was that the emergency?" I asked.

"His blood pressure dropped and he was a little delusional," she said. "The doctor recommended switching him to another medication, which would also help him sleep better. Poor Gustavo," she added, a slight tremor in her voice.

"Yes," I said, and despite myself felt a lump in my throat.

"Did he tell you something?"

"He told me that he was playing chess with one of his neighbors. He suspected he was cheating, though he didn't know how; he was investigating. Then he asked me how you were. Whether you've already taken your exams; you know that he always asks me that or something related to your studies. Otherwise, he's in good shape. The nurses tell me that he eats well and exercises."

"What news, you?"

I told her what I'd found.

"I'm glad you found the bargueño's certificate of authenticity," Tía Astrid said. I gave it up for lost. I'd forgotten that it was Miranda who signed it. Take photos of everything and send them to me soon. I remember the article; I helped them write it. It came out in an academic journal, a thousand years ago, how time goes by."

"And the photos?" she asked.

"I'm sending them to you right now. The last one features my biological great-grandfather, Rafael Ruiz, the artisan, botanist, and adventurer. And three of his daughters," I added after a short pause. I imagined Tía Astrid staring at the blurred photo.

"You have three great-aunts, and probably several second uncles and second cousins!"

"The one in the middle looks like a ghost," I said. When the photo was taken she was shaking her head, as if saying: not yet!"

"The one on the left looks shocked, you would think by something on the back of the taracea inlay frame," Tía Astrid commented. "The three daughters admiring their father's work," she ventured with a trace of irony.

"And the one on the right doesn't seem to have pupils in her eyes," I said.

"She looks like your dad!"

"Do you think?" I asked skeptically and searched for one of Dad's pictures when he was young on my laptop, I had not seen it in a while. He was standing next to my grandmother Francisca, on the day of his First Communion. Seeing the pictures side to side, I had the uncanny feeling of seeing the woman with the faded pupils, one of my biological great-aunts, in my father's face.

"The nose and the mouth were the same," I burst out.

"It's like I was seeing your father when we were kids," Tía Astrid said after a short pause. I'll ask Don Aldemar about your great aunts tomorrow; I hope he has pictures. He's very concerned about your dad, by the way. He wants to come to Bogotá and meet him. He is a very sweet man, you know?"

"What do you think of the taracea works?"

"I see it and I don't believe it, Tía Astrid muttered."

"Do you recognize something?"

"The display table. I know it. I've seen it somewhere. Yes. It could very well be. I have to ask the old man Carrizosa. If I'm not mistaken, he has one like that; although I am inclined to think that this is it; it's a very special piece of furniture. I doubt that it's a reproduction, though, with pirate restorers like Rosiñol del Valle, aka Carlos Cárdenas, you never know. I just remembered that it has an interesting history. He told it to me a long time ago at your grandfather's antique store in Bogotá. According to old man Carrizosa, his grandfather Don Alberto had it made or bought it, I no longer remember, to store and display some old books, family heirlooms, among which, if I'm not mistaken, there was, or is, a sixteenth century illuminated bestiary. Not a facsimile like the one Rosiñol del Valle stole from us but an original, though I'm not sure which."

"All roads lead to Rafael Ruiz, artist, botanist, and adventurer."

You hit the nail on it, Francisco. But it doesn't surprise me much. We know there were very few taracea masters in Bogotá back in the day. Even today," she added wistfully. "It's a shame the tradition will likely die out in a few years. There are only two people in Bogotá that I know of who could manufacture pieces like that. But they only do copies; they're not real artists.

"The bestiary could be the key to reading the bargueño."

"Too bad your grandfather didn't get it back," Tía Astrid commented in a meditative tone. I imagined her sitting in her reclining chair, a glass of scotch in hand, looking through the window at the sprawling western suburbs beyond; it was her midnight ritual. "By the way, do you know what's under the table?"

"Don't tell me it's the bargueño…"

"He had not yet finished it; he still had to put the feet or do the animal engravings; otherwise, he would have put it up facing the person who took the picture. It's not a good image, but I think the length of the bargueño is about the width of the display table, about a meter and a half, I would say."

"You're right, Tía. I'm looking at mine from the side. It is the same design. It's odd that he would show it unfinished."

"Not at all, Francisco. We don't know why the photo was taken. It wasn't for a catalog, that's for sure. It could be just to commemorate the last day that the works were in the hands of their creator. Perhaps he had to deliver the display table and the frame on that day and the bargueño later."

TWENTY-FIVE

Professor Rodrigues arrived just as Ana was leaving; there was barely enough time for introductions. They shook hands and said, at the same time, nice to meet you. Ana was late for an appointment with Natalia to discuss the final paper for one of their classes; they read and commented on each other's work ever since they met.

Rodrigues remarked on the pleasant coincidence that I lived in Tudor City, near the United Nations headquarters building, one of the settings for one of his favorite films, *Two Men in Manhattan*, a Jean-Pierre Melville noir from the late fifties.

I told him I also liked that film and showed him the DVD I had on the bookcase.

"Is that why you chose this neighborhood?"

"A mere coincidence," I replied.

"Do you like jazz?"

"Yes, though I'm not a connoisseur. I've been playing the Martial Solal CD with songs from the Melville movie more often since moving into this apartment."

I asked him if he would like something to drink and he said coffee would be nice. While I was preparing it, we talked a bit more about jazz. He told me about some bands from Europe and Asia that he had seen live in Tokyo. Apparently, most of the big names in the jazz world consider Tokyo to be one of the most important venues. From the way he talked about his nightly tours of jazz clubs, I got the impression that Rodrigues lived a solitary life.

When we sat on the sofa facing the bookcase and the bargueño, I inquired about life for a Colombian in Tokyo.

"As easy or as complicated as in New York," he replied. "It depends on who you are and what you do. But it's not difficult to live in Japan; if you behave well, you go unnoticed, nobody bothers you; salaries are good, and it's easy to get what you want. You can get a resident visa if you get a job at a good company. The Latin American immigrant community is relatively small and diverse, mostly of Japanese origin, and there's already a good number of second, even third-generation, who are for the most part bicultural, like you."

"You have to go, Francisco," he added in a more formal tone. "You should see for yourself. I could recommend you to our Dean for a research grant, when you finish your dissertation, of course. Also, a good friend of mine, a Brazilian sociologist has been researching the Latino community in Tokyo and could help you out."

"Thanks," I said, a bit overwhelmed. I had never considered a research project outside of the U.S. I'd read a couple of articles about Latin Americans in Japan, but they weren't on topics that interested me; I didn't even mention them in the papers I had to write before my research proposal. I would have to read them again.

"I'll send you information about research grants so you can see for yourself," Rodrigues added.

You're very kind, I said almost reflexively; it was a very mom and dad expression from faraway memories.

Rodrigues smiled and bowed his head slightly.

"Do you mind if I take pictures of the engravings?" he asked, his gaze fixed on the bargueño, he had been staring at it while were talking.

"As many as you need," I replied.

While he was taking the photos, he asked me whether I knew if Vartatian and Salazar had a bargueño like mine, though without animal engravings and tortoiseshell inlay plates.

"I understand they bought one in Bogotá a few years ago."

"I found out over the weekend," Rodrigues said. "They invited me to lunch and showed it to me. They have a house in Brooklyn decorated with handicrafts from various regions of Colombia. Do you know the story of how they bought it?"

"I only know that they bought it from a relative or an acquaintance and that it's not an antique."

"I'll tell you the whole story," Rodrigues said and sat back on the sofa. "It may be helpful. A cousin of Marta Salazar, her name is Aurora, who is an actress, also a playwright, wrote a play inspired by some photos of her great-grandmother, from the early twentieth century. In several of the photos, the great-grandmother is surrounded by female relatives and friends, sitting on an *estrado doméstico*, a wooden platform, covered with rugs, cushions, and pillows, and with some furniture, a couple of short tables, and a bargueño. This type of feminine space was a custom of yesteryear, of the ancient

Al-Andalus from the time of the Muslim rule in Iberia. The play itself was a comedy of customs about her great-grandmother's gatherings with relatives and friends on her elegant *estrado*, drinking coffee or herbal teas, chatting about their lives, those of their husbands and their children, with humor and mischief. With very little funding and with a stage set made of cardboard, the play was performed in a small neighborhood theater in La Soledad –what a coincidence, I spent my entire life in Colombia in that neighborhood. The play was so successful that she was invited to present her play in a larger well-established theater. Because she had adequate financing, Aurora had the stage and the furniture made, including the bargueño in the photos. One of her friends knew a master craftsman in La Candelaria who had experience restoring taracea furniture, and he said to her: 'Oh, what a coincidence, that is a bargueño made by the person who taught me so he made one just like the one in the picture.' The only different thing was the lateral inlays which were made of faux tortoiseshell; you couldn't use the real thing, it was banned to protect the tortoises. When the season came to an end, Aurora decided to sell it; she needed the money; she didn't like the style either, she lived in a modern apartment with contemporary décor. Marta found out about it and bought it for the same price Aurora paid for it. A year later, before returning to the United States, a well-known antique dealer offered to purchase it for three times that amount. The master craftsman who made it passed away, and in Bogotá, or perhaps in the entire country, no one knew the taracea craft well enough. But Marta and Vartatian decided that perhaps in

New York they could get a better offer. If they decided to sell it, they knew they had a small treasure in their hands."

"Do you think that the master craftsman was my grandfather Rafael Ruiz?" I asked.

"I don't think so," Rodrigues replied. "The marquetry is not very good; there are many errors, and the engravings, although well done, are repeated floral motifs –there is nothing special."

"Perhaps he made it in a hurry," I ventured.

"It is possible, of course," Rodrigues said, scratching his temple. "But your grandfather was a true master; I doubt he would make something of that low quality. All in all, the bargueño is not that bad; someone who doesn't know taracea work –or your grandfather and great-grandfather's work– might think that it's a well-made piece. From what I heard, taracea works no longer have a discerning audience in Bogotá; people's tastes have changed and the Spanish heritage is not as attractive as other styles. To make matters worse, I have been told that there is no public or private entity in charge of preserving the taracea craft in all of Colombia, and without financial support it is not viable as a business. In Spain, things are different, of course, but that's *harina de otro costal*, another kettle of fish."

"I didn't know you were so interested in the subject," I said, smiling to myself. *Harina de otro costal* translated as flour from another sack, and it always sounded funny to me. Dad sometimes used that expression to express disagreement or his flat-out rejection of something. I remembered that he used the expression on the last day we went to Natsuko. We had already come home and I kept teasing him about the romance that I was beginning to imagine he had with Noriko-san, the slender elegant woman who owned the restaurant. *Harina de otro costal*, he'd said curtly to put an end to my teasing.

"My first degree was in the history of colonial art in Latin America," Rodrigues said, his gaze still on the bargueño. "It's a long story, but I'll give you the Reader's Digest version: for my graduate studies, I shifted my focus to the old continent, and from there, for my dissertation, to the expansion of the Portuguese empire and the Catholic Church in Asia. That was the path that led me to Japan."

"My parents studied art history at St. Xavier's," I said almost without thinking; I instantly regretted it.

"Oh really? Are they the ones in the photo, next to the bargueño?"

I nodded but felt uncomfortable.

"What year did they graduate?" Rodrigues asked.

"In eighty-two. One year before I was born."

"I graduated in eighty-one," Rodrigues said and lowered his gaze, perhaps trying to remember something. "Perhaps we took some classes together," he added. I had a feeling that he was going to ask for their names, but he returned his gaze to the photo of Mom and Dad, they were in front of the university library. They were both smiling, but in a formal way, a conventional pose, like a studio portrait.

After a pause in which he savored what was left of his cup of coffee, Rodrigues commented that before coming to New York he spent two weeks in Andalusia on vacation. "I spoke with several taracea masters in Granada and Córdoba who told me that every day there is less interest in this kind of work," he went on, with some emphasis, dragging the R's, like my grandfather Gustavo used to.

"Most of the shops are still in business because they sell souvenirs, small jewelry boxes, cup holders, chess boards, and the like. A master craftsman, owner of one of the shops along one of the streets that runs down from the Alhambra Palace to the center of the city in Granada, told me that years ago he sold on average four or five bargueños a year. But for some time now, very few people even show an interest, perhaps because of their high price tag; they require many hours of specialized work."

"I showed him the photos I have of the bargueño that belongs to your second cousin, and after examining them he told me that it was made in the unique Granada style. He noted that if I hadn't told him they were the work of a Colombian artisan, he would have thought it was the work of his grandfather or great-grandfather."

"Did he say something about the engravings?"

"Yes," Rodrigues replied. "He said they probably contained a message. According to him, the engravings referred to the trade and social position of the people who had them made. Also, sometimes they had built-in secret compartments where documents, jewelry, and other relics were kept. Yours isn't big enough for a secret compartment —but it harbors a story or a family secret," he concluded.

TWENTY-SIX

Ana returned around ten, said she was worn out, and ran a bubble bath. I was working on my laptop, hoping to craft the introduction to my dissertation –a theoretical essay on literature and ethnographic writing, an extension of my research proposal with an exhaustive literature review, encompassing books, articles, and conference proceedings. Despite it being my chosen research topic and knowing the literature well, that night I struggled to make the text flow as I desired; the sentences seemed inaccurate and flat. Besides, other thoughts lingered in my mind. Rodrigues' visit had left me somewhat intrigued. I had the vague impression that there was something behind his offer to help me with my project, although I couldn't imagine what it might be. I had the fanciful idea that he was writing a noir novel set in Manhattan jazz clubs, where I was a character in possession of an important object that others desired; a plot akin to *The Maltese Falcon*, a classic Hollywood movie I've always liked.

After her bath, Ana came to my side, kissed my forehead. She wore her floral print Kimono robe and was barefoot, on her body the scent of chamomile flowers.

"I saw your new friend Rodrigues again, after class," she said and sat next to me. He was in Vartatian's office with an

Asian woman, a human rights lawyer. They were leaving; they had a meeting with the Dean, and we barely had time to say hi.

"Sounds intriguing," I mused. What is it about?

"A few things darling," said Ana. "The first is that your friend Rodrigues is helping the Academic Affairs Committee write a proposal to restructure the Department of Historical and Social Studies. He said the idea was to add some of the courses that could be accepted as electives in the Anthropology and Sociology program on historiography and historical methods, as well as workshops on ethnographic writing. I think it's a great idea, Natalia and Ricardo think the same. What do you think?"

"Look who you're asking," I said.

"The other thing," Ana continued, arching her eyebrows, "is that Rodrigues is applying for a visiting professor position in that department."

"A very clever move on his part," I remarked.

Vartatian told me that if everything goes well, that is, if the committee accepts the proposal, perhaps they may even offer Rodrigues a full-time position.

"In which case there would be two Colombians with voting power in the Graduate School," I noted.

Ana smiled and raised her eyebrows again.

"And what does the Asian woman have to do with Rodrigues?"

"Ah, the Asian woman. You won't believe it, but she is Rodrigues's daughter."

"Is she Japanese?"

"No," said Ana. "She is Dutch and of Indonesian-Chinese origin. Your friend has a very colorful past. Vartatian knows everything about him because they have known each other for some time."

"They were backpacking in Indonesia when they were graduate students," I said. "Rodrigues told me that Vartatian and Marta Salazar met in a restaurant or bar, I don't remember, but he didn't tell me anything else."

"He didn't tell you the main thing, which is interesting and consequential," Ana commented. "It turns out that the girlfriend he was traveling with never told him that she had become pregnant. She returned to her country, married another man with whom she raised her daughter, and she never said anything to Rodrigues. Twenty-five years later, when he was on vacation in Goa, India, he saw a woman on the beach, a young woman, who was the living image of that girlfriend, and realized that she could be his daughter. But she told him that it was not possible because her father was a Goan doctor of Portuguese ancestry who by coincidence resembled him."

"Sounds like a soap opera to me," I said.

"Thanks to DNA testing," Ana went on, "she confirmed that he was her father. He is also the passive carrier of a genetic disease; though different from yours."

"Really?" I asked, surprised.

"Synchronicity," Ana said.

"Did Vartatian trust you with all this?"

"He told me that this was the beginning of a novel that Rodrigues published a couple of years ago."

"I have to read it," I said and pointed to the copy I had checked out from the library.

"It's funny that you two are carriers," Ana commented, holding her chin in one hand with her elbow on the table.

"And that the truth has been hidden from us."

"It was hidden from your grandfather."

"Both grandfathers, I corrected."

"Those were the times," Ana said ironically.

"All of this is somewhat overwhelming: a new family, a parallel history, and a DNA profile with nasty surprises."

"We'll sort it all out," Ana said and got up.

"Sleep well cariño," I said.

"I love it when you call me cariño, Francisco."

I detected a trace of desire in her words and I took her hand. I tried to pull her towards me, but she took a step back. She winked at me, and whispered: "I'm spent, but we'll talk about manna from heaven tomorrow, deal?"

"Whatever," I said and stuck my tongue out at her, what she would have done in my case.

I returned my eyes to my laptop, to the writings that would start the academic career that I would perhaps do with Ana by my side or the other way round; she would also be a colleague, as in the case of Vartatian and Marta Salazar, in some way like Mom and Dad. I had plenty of time to think about that.

I read the text in front of me, a paragraph on the impossibility of writing and the limits of language. However, the sentences seemed imprecise and hollow to me. I changed one of the phrases from passive to active, but it instantly sounded wrong and I deleted it. I read three paragraphs back and nothing sounded right to me. I couldn't write like that.

TWENTY-SEVEN

I met Alejandra, Ana's cousin —who reminded me of the evil girl from the soap opera I used to watch with Mom— at Starbucks, near Rockefeller Center. She called me when I was leaving the university to tell me that she had some information about my bargueño she wanted to share in person, she didn't give me any more details, only said it was urgent.

"Thanks for coming," she told me, in Spanish after we sat at the coffee bar, facing the street. "Today I had to write a report about a bargueño like yours," Alejandra said, with some emphasis.

"With the same engravings? I asked," surprised.

"Everything is the same, including the anti-Semitic owl," Alejandra replied, and she took off the scarf she was wearing; it was just like the one Ana had, a souvenir of Aunt Margarita's trip to Mongolia. Underneath it, Alejandra was wearing a blouse and a kind of tie made of the same material that gave her an executive, Wall Street look.

"It was requested by our purchasing department, she went on. A client in Manhattan who has an extensive collection of Latin American colonial art is selling it to us."

"Do you know who?" I asked and had to cough; my throat was suddenly dry.

"We don't have a name; we always deal with a lawyer who acts on his or her behalf, it's someone who prefers to remain anonymous," she explained.

I asked her whether it was an antique.

She replied technically not. "The skeleton is of recent manufacture, ten years maximum," she commented, "but the moldings and veneers are old, from the nineteen twenties or thirties. They removed the original veneers and replaced them with the old ones."

"To make it more valuable," I ventured.

"We have a client in Dubai who pays good money for taracea colonial art."

I was going to say that I had a second cousin who lived in Dubai, but I decided not to. There was no point in telling her, at least not now.

"Could you send me the photos of your bargueño?" Alejandra asked. "I would like to double-check something. If you don't mind, of course," she added in a friendly tone and smiled.

"Sure," I said and searched for the photos on my mobile. When I was done sending the files, I had a strange feeling that it was not I who was there but someone who was watching closely.

As Alejandra examined the photos, I couldn't help but admire how her straight dark hair fell at a slant to her shoulders; it had a soft bluish glow. I noticed that her eyebrows were carefully outlined and her eyelashes were long and thick; in that she resembled Ana.

"Good work," Alejandra said in a low voice after a few moments, as if to herself. "The craftsman copied the engravings from yours, probably traced them, to use them over and over again. But I doubt that it is the same person. If I remember correctly, yours was made in the nineteen thirties or forties, and this one was made about fifteen years ago, in the early two thousands; there are at least six decades in between. Maybe it was someone who learned from him, or her."

"One of his sons," I proposed.

"Or an apprentice. Do you want to eat something?" Alejandra asked suddenly. "I'm going to get a sandwich; I haven't eaten anything all day."

I said no and thanked her, and Alejandra got up and in three swift strides, she went over to the cashier, made her order, and paid. Seeing that, I thought the executive outfit she was wearing was a costume, like Clark Kent's.

"There is more," Alejandra remarked when she came back. "The same client also offered us a facsimile of an illuminated manuscript from the 16th century: the bestiary of Don Juan de Austria, published in Burgos in 1830. As you can imagine, I was startled. I'm not in charge of the appraisal, but I took a look at it. All the animal engravings on the bargueño drawers are copied from the manuscript. I have a soft copy of it," she added, in a tone of confidence. "If you are interested, I'll send it to you."

I said of course and thanked her. The feeling that it was not I but another watching close by grew sharper. Something in Alejandra's way, her behavior, and the way she spoke altered me, upset my equilibrium. Perhaps it was because she was attractive– or because I was attracted to her. Or both. Or perhaps because her confidential tone of voice was an indication that she already saw me as part of her circle or her family, something that would take me much longer. Whatever it was, she also made me feel a bit guilty, as if our conversation was a prelude to a romantic affair or something of that nature.

"Is the engraving in the center the same?" I asked, trying to overcome my discomfort.

"Yes and no," Alejandra replied. "The engraving of the bargueño I examined is the same, but it has fewer lines and shadows, which makes it easier to search with a Reverse Image Search. At work, we have a Facial Recognition app with which we can compare drawings and photographs. Up to now, I've found similarities in various engravings and drawings of notable medieval Andalusians. The one with the highest percentage of strokes in common is a tenth-century drawing of Al-Zahrawi, also known as Albucasis, a famous Cordoba-born Muslim doctor, considered the father of modern surgery. This information could help you. As you may know, the engravings in old bargueños were related to the office or position of whoever commissioned their making. We could speculate that one of your ancestors was a descendant of Moors from the Iberian Peninsula who migrated to the New World ...

Alejandra was about to go on but she held back and stared at something across the street, her brow slightly furrowed. I looked in the same direction but did not see anything special: across the street was a large Nintendo store, with a huge Super Mario golden statue visible through one of its windows. I had been there once with Angela, who was very fond of video games, even in high school; I no longer played by then. A black Mercedes Benz SUV with tinted windows was parked in front of the store. Two men were talking in the car. One of them was a young Arab who wore a white robe with a round collar and on his head a red and white checked scarf held by a kind of crown-shaped rope. I assumed that it was an entrepreneur or business executive from the Persian Gulf, I had read something recently about the bustling economy of those countries. The other man of European looks wore a suit and a tie and carried an executive briefcase.

"He's the lawyer," Alejandra said, after a few moments, and typed something on her mobile. "The other man, the one wearing the white robe, must be a client from Dubai." Alejandra discreetly took photos of the scene; as a reflex action I did the same, it occurred to me that it would help me.

"Are they closing the deal today?" I asked.

"No, we are just beginning the negotiations," Alejandra replied, and she looked at her mobile, which had vibrated. Meanwhile, the man in the tunic got into the Mercedes, and the lawyer turned the corner heading north, towards Rockefeller Center Plaza, where the main entrance to Christie's was.

"Shouldn't you be there?" I asked.

"My boss is waiting for him," Alejandra replied and put her mobile back in her bag.

"Can you tell me how much the bargueño would sell for?"

"I'm not the one who decides the exact price," Alejandra replied, and she combed her bangs with her fingers; for an instant, she glanced at me. "As you can imagine, there are other factors to take into account," she went on, her gaze fixed on the Mercedes still parked across the street. "It could be in the six figures, including the bestiary, of course."

TWENTY-EIGHT

Dear Francisco, You don't know how pleased I am to meet you even by email. My apologies for not replying sooner. I have been traveling a lot in recent months for personal and work matters. I am back in Madrid but in a few days, I will travel again, first to Bogotá to meet our cousin Adriana and to do the transfer of ownership of the bargueño. I will be the new owner and as far as I am concerned, it will always remain in the family, I have no intention of selling it in the future. Three weeks after that, I'll be in New York to attend the annual Historical Society conference, which lasts a week, the last of the month. If you happen to be in town during that time, perhaps we could meet.

As Professor Rodrigues mentioned to you, I am investigating the genealogy of our common family. First, let me explain how we are related. Our common ancestor is Rafael Ruiz Gutierrez, born in 1890, who was married twice. You and Adriana descend from the line of the first marriage with Soledad Herrera, and I from the second, with Maria Valenzuela. In this genealogical chart are the lines of descent.

As you can see, our great-grandfather only had one child with Soledad Herrera, Rafael Ruiz Herrera, your biological grandfather, who had a child out of wedlock with Francisca

Riaño, Gustavo Torres, your father. After that, he married Carmen Rodriguez with whom he had two children, Aldemar, your biological uncle, and Adriana's father, your cousin. The youngest was named Javier, he ran away from home when he was eighteen, and apparently, he died of malaria in the Amazon region. It is interesting that you mentioned the magazine article published in 1947 about our great-grandfather. That was my starting point. This was almost ten years ago, before moving to Madrid. The rumor in the family was that our great-grandfather was born in Tocaima at the end of the 19th century, so I went to the town to search the local civil and religious archives for proof. Unfortunately, I did not find any. I searched the archives of neighboring towns with the same results. Then, I went to the National Archives in Bogotá but I didn't find a trace of him either. It is possible that his documents have been lost or that he changed his name, our great-grandfather was an adventurous youth. In the magazine article, he claims that he spent time in a penal colony, but I have not been able to verify it, I'm still searching, but the dates do not fit. In the last few months, I have been in contact with people who knew him personally, the owners of a well-known antique store in Bogotá. They told me something I didn't know: our great-grandfather did restoration work for state museums and the former presidential palace the San Carlos mansion. I contacted the archivists of those museums and the presidential palace, but it was useless, they had no information about the restorers they employed before the reorganization of the museum in the nineteen eighties. It is very interesting what you tell me about the theft and the return of the copy of the bargueño, and, of

Rosiñol del Valle aka Carlos Cárdenas. I will see what I can find about him in Bogotá. I will meet with the curators and heads of the museum archives, and with the owners of the antique store I mentioned earlier. Interestingly, that antique shop, Casa Izquierdo, has on its website a couple of bargueños for sale that may well be the work of our great-grandfather or perhaps of one of his children or an apprentice not related to the family. I will keep you posted. In the attached document, I answered the question you asked me in your second email. It so happens it is part of the Introduction of a book I am writing about our great-grandfather and the making of the Arca de Noé bargueño.

Sincerely, Sara Ruiz, your third cousin.

The document was a first-person account of how she was hired as a professor and researcher of Ibero-American Colonial Art at a university in Madrid. Following was an account of her arrival in Granada, the first stop in a two-week trip through Andalusia before traveling to Madrid to start her work.

To my great surprise, at the hotel reception, there was a bargueño like the one I have in my living room, of more or less the same size and design, six drawers in two rows on the sides, and a large drawer in the middle with an engraved bone plate of floral designs. I asked the receptionist and he told me that they had bought it in a taracea workshop and store, not far from there, on the street that goes up to the Alhambra Palace. After unpacking my luggage and taking a shower, I visited the workshop and store. I met the owner, a tall, middle-aged man with gray hair, named Buendía. He told me that the hotel's bargueño was his work. I showed him some photos of my bargueño and he told me that the person who made it was well acquainted with the old granaíno taracea style, which few practiced anymore, including him and some of his relatives. It was a unique style, with an emphasis on bone engravings of various motifs –not the geometric mosaics typical of Mudéjar art, which were popular with tourists.

That night I got the sad news that my dear grandfather Gilberto had passed away. Aside from the pain it caused me, the news also made me think that the cogs of the universe were taking me down the path I had to travel in my search for my roots. First, I came across a bargueño that looked like a cherished family heirloom at the hotel's reception, upon my arrival in this ancient city, a scenario of medieval splendor, a melting pot of cultures. Then the conversation with the owner of the taracea workshop and store about the particularity of the granaíno style of which my bargueño was an example; and then the sad news of the passing of who best knew and appreciated that work of art.

One day when I was little, Grandfather Gilberto told me the story of the bargueño – It is remarkable how memories link to one another. He told me that it was not an antique, but a copy of one from the seventeenth century, inherited from an illustrious ancestor. His father, my great-grandfather, commissioned his making to replace the original that he had donated to the recently established Museo del Virreinato in Bogotá.

The taracea master to whom the great-grandfather commissioned that work was someone who rumor had it was a distant relative, someone from humble origins, taracea and other kinds of woodworking were working-class trades. Be that as it may, the copy was of such perfection that no one remembered that it was not the valuable seventeenth-century antique that had been passed on as a family heirloom.

TWENTY-NINE

A waning moon had risen over the East River. I opened the sliding doors to the balcony, went to the kitchen, and poured myself a glass of scotch on the rocks. I thought of my odd meeting with Alejandra that afternoon.

She called me before lunch and asked if I had time to see some pieces of colonial art that they had just acquired and would soon put on sale, which in her opinion could be the work of the taracea master who made the bargueño that we discussed the other day, and perhaps of mine as well, unlikely as that possibility was. There's something strange going on, she confided and told me that the client from Dubai was very interested and was coming to look at the pieces in a couple of days. I told her that I would drop by late afternoon.

When I got to Christie's, a guard took me to one of the building's basements, where there was a warehouse and several conference rooms. Alejandra, who that day was wearing a pantsuit with a tie, was talking on her mobile and gestured me to go to a large room at the back, where I understood they stored the pieces she'd mentioned. To my great surprise, in the middle of the room was a taracea display table like the one in the photos attached to the certificate of authenticity of my bargueño. I opened the copies I'd made of those pictures and confirmed it. It was the same table! It was in perfect condition, although upon close inspection some of the wood veneers and bone plates had small horizontal cracks that showed the passage of time. Overall, it was an elegant and well-balanced piece of furniture, with a certain shine to it, the patina of a precious object, meticulously cared for over time. The marquetry work was similar to the one in my bargueño with engraved bone plates and tortoiseshell veneers, it was an amazing table, I couldn't take my eyes off it. The other works were on a work table with professional photography spotlights on them. They were also taracea pieces: two wooden crosses with tortoiseshell veneers, Christs in silver, and rare *gota de aceite* emeralds embedded on a silver base; two small estrado tables; and a bargueño in Mudéjar style with geometric motifs.

After her conversation ended, Alejandra entered the room and commented in a matter-of-fact professional tone that the works looked to be the same age as my bargueño, although they had been restored more than once, and just as in the case of the bargueño she'd examined the week before, some of the marquetry pieces were very likely older, perhaps from the nineteen thirties or forties. She asked me not to take photos, she would send me the ones they were going to use for the assessment protocol. It took me a few moments to realize that Alejandra was speaking to me in English, it was the first time that I heard her speak it, she was completely fluent with just a trace of an accent. Despite myself, I felt attracted to her again. In a tone that sounded casual, but somehow seemed calculated, she invited me to have a cappuccino in one of the conference rooms; she said there we could talk in private. Once we sat down, and in the same confident tone that she had used in the cafe a few days ago –this time in English– she asked me what my theory was about the origin of the works that we had just seen. I took a sip of the cappuccino and decided to tell her everything, starting with the theft of the bargueño and its mysterious return. Alejandra didn't seem too surprised with the twists and turns, perhaps Ana had already told her the story. After a short pause, she said that if it was indeed Carlos Cárdenas who was making or restoring the pieces in the collection, she and other staff would have to investigate. The lawyer representing the seller mentioned that the pieces belonged to an old Bogotá family.

On the way home, I fantasized about meeting Alejandra again, this time at a Jazz bar in the Village, where John Coltrane, miraculously alive, played music we both liked. It was a scenario I had also imagined with Ana when we first started going out. It was a pity that Ana did not appreciate Coltrane or jazz in general; she told me again and again that she didn't get that kind of geometry. I would say that I understood but I never really did, sometimes this happens to me in Spanish, I understand all the words but not always their nuances.

The insistent wail of an ambulance's siren brought me out of my musings; it rushed fast down the avenue behind our building. I opened my computer and searched the Internet for the actress who played the role of the evil girl in the Colombian series that I used to watch with Mom. She would now be about Tía Astrid's age, five or six years younger than Dad. I found a website with pictures of her playing different characters throughout her career. I stared at one that took my fancy in which her hair fell to her shoulder but it wasn't dark with a bluish tint but light brown, perhaps its original color. All at once Diane Keaton's Annie Hall came to mind, her smile both enigmatic and seductive. I closed my eyes and saw her singing Seems Like Old Times, the song that Dad liked so much. Mom too, it was she who hummed to it when we would listen to Ella Fitzgerald's version. I heard the final line: *Seems like old times here with you*, which also plays at the end of the film, a bittersweet scene of a romance that wouldn't work according to the narrator, whose monologue we heard at the same time as the end of the song; a stereophonic epilogue for two voices.

What was I thinking? That Annie Hall would be the script of my relationship with Alejandra? That such would be its arc? That it wouldn't last?

I played the movie on my computer; I watched it once or twice a year. Ana didn't care for Woody Allen's movies, she was appalled that I did, and once told me that I would eventually see the error of my ways. I couldn't argue with her about it. For me, Annie Hall was a sort of time machine that would take me back to the many times I would watch with Dad. It was sort of a ritual that bonded us together, also with Mom, to her memory...

A voice woke me up suddenly. It was Ana who had sat next to me. She was telling me something about a dinner that I didn't understand.

"Did you already have dinner," she asked.

"I was waiting for you," I replied and rubbed my eyes.

"I brought pizza and a bottle of good wine, I splurged a little."

"Are we celebrating something?"

"I hope so," she replied and went to the kitchen.

"You leave me hanging."

"Ascuas!" Ana exclaimed.

"I don't know what you are talking about."

"Nothing, I burned myself a little, ascuas means embers," Ana said and placed two scented candles on the table.

"I was permitted to work at the Hispanic Society this summer," Ana said as we sat down to eat. "The board of directors agreed to give me access to their archives to investigate the narrative structure of the exhibitions that have been made of Spanish art in the last twenty years. I told Vartatian and he thought it was great. He even suggested that I could begin my dissertation with a critical discussion on the cultural hybridity of the Iberian Middle Ages and its influence on the formulation of the national in Latin America. I told him that was exactly what I wanted to do, and thanked him for the go-ahead. If I win the scholarship from the Anthropology Association we could go to Mexico and Colombia next summer, maybe also to Ecuador and Peru, I don't know ..."

"What do you think?"

"It could be," I said, perhaps without much conviction.

Ana made a face of surprise. "I have the impression that you are mad at me. Is that?"

"No, Ana, it's not that."

"I'm aware I've been a little distant the last few weeks," Ana went on. "I've been very nervous about my proposal, but with Natalia's help, I had a breakthrough and I'm now confident I'll have it done in a few weeks. Also, there is a bit of family drama that shouldn't matter so much to me, but for some reason it has, I don't know why."

"Did something happen to your parents in Colombia?" I asked.

"No, my dear pirata," she replied and frowned slightly. "It's about Alejandra. Mehrdad was offered a full-time position at the University of Macao and he is very enthusiastic about the offer, he says that the salary is great plus he'll get subsidized housing and round-trip tickets to New York two times a year, not to mention the research funds that will be made available to him."

"But Alejandra doesn't want to go," I said.

"You hit on the nail, Francisco. She's being foolish and difficult. She says that the move would be a setback, she would have to start from scratch, not to mention she'll have to learn another language."

"Does Christie's have a branch in Macau?"

"In Hong Kong, which is next door, but for Princess Alejandra, an hour's journey by ferry and taking public transportation is a cross too heavy to bear. She was born to have a chauffeur to take her everywhere, in Manhattan, of course. To top it all, my cousin is a bit of a racist, I'm so sorry to tell you."

"Do you know that for sure?"

"Of course, I do, she replied and took another sip of wine. She is my cousin and I love her very much, but since I was a child I have heard her make derogatory comments about people of color. Even now, though not when there's anyone else within earshot. I remember that at the party they had for her before she left for boarding school in Switzerland, she asked Aunt Margarita not to allow one of her maids, a black girl, with whom Jacobo was in love, to serve the food or drinks that day. She claimed that she would *spoil the photographs*. She later explained to me in her arrogant princess-know-it-all tone that she was an *esthete*, that she didn't tolerate ugliness, and that she just couldn't help it."

"And what did you say?"

"What could I have said? I chuckled it off."

"You are a little evil, I said."

"I'm not, you know that."

"That's ancient history,' I noted, in a lighter tone.

"Alejandra hasn't changed much, I can assure you."

"Is Mehrdad very handsome?" I hastened to ask. I didn't want to discuss how much or how little people change over time. Ana and I stand on opposite sides of that issue.

"A dandy worse than D'Artagnan," Ana replied. "He's a French man out of the seventies, a la Jean-Paul Belmondo: very suave , wears the best colognes and dresses impeccably, also very polite, only drives Mercedes Benz or other German cars, convertibles, preferably. The two make a per-fect match. But I don't want to talk about this little drama. You don't know how distressed Aunt Margarita has been with Alejandra's attitude. I just want to tell you that I'm sorry I've been a little distant. I don't want anything to draw us apart. Shall we toast to that?"

THIRTY

While I waited for Ana, Natalia, and Ricardo at the bar in *Tierra Natal*, Fernando, the bartender, asked me how I knew Angela. He'd seen me having dinner with her and her father several times in the last few weeks. He told me that he'd known her since they were little, they went to grade school together in Jackson Heights. I told him, I had known her since high school. After shaking hands, he mentioned that Angela said I was interviewing them for a research project.

I explained that I wasn't going to use their real names and would only disclose what they were comfortable with.

"Maybe we met once," Fernando ventured after a short silence in which he looked me in the eye. "At Angela's graduation party at her home in Long Island," he explained.

I squinted my eyes searching for that memory and asked if he was the one who rolled the joint in the game room in the basement.

Fernando nodded sheepishly and smiled. I then remembered we'd chatted about something, perhaps our plans for the future.

"That day I got in trouble with my old man," he commented and crossed his arms. A few weeks after that party, on my eighteenth birthday, I joined the United States

Marine Corps. It was something that I had already contemplated, so it was not a big surprise for my family. I spent four years on active duty at the Yokosuka Naval Base in Japan. I liked the jobs assigned to me at the base, especially with the communication teams, though little by little I realized that military life, the routine, taking orders, and all of that was not for me, so I left. It's not easy leaving the Marines, I mean the paperwork, but I managed an honorable discharge."

I asked him what coming back to New York had been like, more out of politeness than out of genuine interest. I had the impression that Fernando was telling me this with an ulterior motive; it occurred to me that he was in love with Angela. Or perhaps Fernando was like that, and he would tell anyone who had a beer at his bar on a slow night the story of his life straight from the shoulder.

"I didn't return right away," Fernando continued in a leisurely tone and poured himself a glass of tonic water from the fountain. I went to live with a Chilean girlfriend I met in a Latin bar in Tokyo. I was with her for a year, although I had to leave the country every three months, which is how long a tourist visa lasts. I worked the bar –under-the-table, of course– in the same Latin club where I met the Chilean girl. She was a hostess at a Japanese bar in the same neighborhood, so we had a similar schedule. Everything was going well until she got another job that paid more, though with daytime hours. From then on, we didn't see each other so much; we hardly went out partying. When the fun ended, the relationship ended. After Japan, I went to the Philippines for three months. Eventually, the money I'd saved ran out and I came back to New York. Mr. Cruz —Angela's father— offered me a job at his furniture factory on thirty-sixth Avenue, where I worked until he decided to sell the business about two years ago, the two years I've been here."

I asked him if he knew the new owner.

"Everyone knows Don Carlos Cárdenas," Fernando commented in an animated tone and pointed at the stuff hanging from the ceiling. "He did the decoration of the restaurant, which has become very famous; it was featured in the New York Times, and some people come just for that. He brought all those things from Colombia; some are antiques, such as kitchen utensils and horse riding gear. The hammock spun with the Colombian flag, and the mannequin sleeping on it is the work of his goddaughter, a young woman from Cali who is doing a law degree at NYU. When Don Carlos comes, he's a guest. But he is very generous and he gives us tips on what he would have spent if he had to pay the bill."

I then inquired if he knew what type of business Cárdenas ran, but at that moment I saw Ana, Natalia, and Ricardo come in. Fernando followed my gaze and said that he had reserved the best table for us at the back, next to the dance floor. "We'll talk some other time, he added."

After greeting Natalia and Ricardo, whom I had not seen for almost a month, they asked me about the interviews with Angela and her father. I summarized them in the best way that I could. I commented that an interesting topic was the attachment that father and daughter had for their life in New York in contrast to their mother and younger sisters who preferred to live in Colombia and had no intention of returning to New York. Both Angela and her father agreed that this arrangement was the only way to keep the family together, an interesting paradox. But the most valuable thing was what the bartender had just told me: Angela's father sold the Cruz family's furniture factory to Carlos Cárdenas, a thief and pirate restorer.

"Do you know when he returns to New York?" Natalia asked.

"A reliable source tells me that he will be back from Dubai in a few days."

"From Dubai? "Ana asked, surprised.

"Your cousin Alejandra sent me a text with the information," I said.

Ana and Natalia looked at each other. Almost as a reflex, I winked at Ricardo.

"Carlos Cárdenas is a very clever man," I said. "He somehow got into the antique business in Dubai, which is booming. According to Sara Ruiz, my third cousin, who has contacts there, there is a sheik who collects art from Al Andalus, where the taracea craft was developed. My bargueño is an example of that, by the way; it was made in the old granaíno style. Apart from his private collection, the sheik is the patron of a cultural center in Dubai and Seville to foster dialogue between Muslims and Christians. He wants to establish a branch in Latin America, perhaps in Colombia. My cousin says that behind that there are commercial interests: the port authority of Dubai, one of the largest in the world, wants to invest in Colombian ports; and the Emirati government is interested in joint mining projects, although I don't know exactly where or what kind of minerals."

"The external reader of your dissertation worked at a university in Dubai for a year," Ricardo commented.

"I didn't know you were on the hiring committee," I said.

"They appointed me last week; Natalia too, they needed a student from the Department of Historical and Social Studies."

"How is Rodrigues as a candidate?" Ana asked.

"He gave a very good presentation on Portuguese imperialism in Asia and the Japanese slave trade, including that of women for prostitution in Portugal in the sixteenth century. He commented that it was for an anthology of comparative studies on slavery in Asia that would include an article that he and a lawyer specializing in human rights were writing about human trafficking in Japan. All the students agreed that he was an excellent candidate."

"But are they hiring him or not?" I asked.

"The dean, Vartatian, Salazar, and the students voted for him; the Japanese sociologist abstained, as did the continental philosopher," Natalia pointed out.

"He starts next semester," Ricardo announced.

The dishes we ordered came one after the other; mine was a red bean casserole, the only Colombian dish that Mom knew how to cook. It was a Sunday dish, and Dad kept up the tradition.

During dinner we talked about Natalia and Ricardo's ideas for research projects; they were one semester behind Ana, two behind me. They both said that given Rodrigues' appointment, they might change their minds and do something related to historical memory. Natalia added that she was very interested in Ana's research on museums and would probably go in that direction. Ricardo jokingly added that in that case, he could join the franchise, so they could go to the same conferences together. I said I would find some topic I could present at such conferences, but after I said it, it sounded awkward and phony. Ana took my hand under the table, perhaps to reassure me. I was happy to see my friends, though my mind was still on Carlos Cárdenas, someone whom I felt had done me wrong but who seemed very popular with everyone I met in Astoria. On the other hand, talking about the future was a topic I preferred to avoid. If I was lucky, I would be finishing my dissertation in a year, and luckier still, if I got a job, even if it was a postdoc or a visiting gig by next September. I couldn't afford to not have a job by then, unlike Ana and my friends who had wealthy families. If Ana and I were still together, the issue would be whether Ana could get a job in the US, which would be made easier if we were married, a topic that had not yet come up. But even if we married, our future depended on the academic job market. Getting jobs in the same university would be ideal but highly unlikely; getting jobs in the same city, a little less.

When they served us dessert, a lemon tart that we were going to share, a *vallenato* song began to play which sounded vaguely familiar. A couple sitting at the bar stepped onto the dance floor.

"We have to dance to this song," Ana declared and got up. Natalia and Ricardo did the same; they liked to dance whenever the opportunity arose. For an instant, I was the only one who didn't move. On my way to the dance floor, I noticed that Fernando, the bartender, was giving us the thumbs up.

While we were dancing, Ana warned me not to get jealous: that *vallenato* song was the favorite of her first lover, a man ten years older than her whom she met on vacation in Palma de Mallorca when she was sixteen or seventeen; a man who had come to the United States from Colombia at a very young age and now lived in Bangkok.

"Do you write to him?" I asked.

"He never wrote me a line," she replied and corrected my step. "Javier wasn't born to be in a relationship," Ana went on. "I kind of thought the same about you when we started to go out, as you well know. I found him by chance while surfing the Net two or three years ago. He has a bilingual blog where he writes about this and that, though mostly about backpacking around the world. He uses the pseudonym Ruiseñor, Nightingale, as in the title of the vallenato we are dancing to, *Ruiseñor de mi valle*, A nightingale from my valley....

THIRTY-ONE

"Is Rosiñol the same as ruiseñor?" I asked when we went back to our table.

"I think so," Ana said.

"I think in all Romance languages," Natalia, speculated. "In Catalan it is written with two 's' and a 'y' at the end: Rossinyol. In French Rossignol with a 'g' and an 'n.'"

"In Portuguese it's with an 'ou' and an 'x': Rouxinol, a male name often shortened to Roux," Ana said, looking at her mobile.

"A nervous bird that sings beautifully," Ricardo quipped.

"I wouldn't have thought it was anything but a last name," I said. "I couldn't recognize the bird or its song. Roux is one of the main characters of Indian Nocturne by Antonio Tabuchi," I blurted without giving it much thought; I was thinking out loud. "It's the story of a man who goes to India to find a friend of his, but it's not clear whether the friend exists at all or is himself," I added a little uncertain.

Ana looked me in the eye and laughed. "You find links to that novel in the most unusual things," she said. "If you allow me," she added in a tone of feigned haughtiness, "I can give you a more relevant connection, and from *real* life. If you had searched the Internet for the title of the song we just danced, *Ruiseñor de mi valle* –Nightingale of My Valley– you would have come across Jorge Oñate, known in musical circles as *El ruiseñor del Cesar* –the Nightingale of Cesar's Department in Colombia– and its capital city Valledupar, in the Upar valley, the land of my grandfather, the world capital of *vallenato* music, which now shares a category with cumbia in the Grammy Awards. We'll have to go one day; it is a very special place."

"Oñate? Is there a surname like that in Spanish?" I asked, more intrigued than amused.

"A Vizcaíno last name, from Euskera, Basque Country," Ricardo explained.

"My last name Aguirre is also from Euskera," Natalia added.

"And Velázquez your second last name," Ana declared, looking at me.

"Was this Oñate popular in Colombia?" I asked.

"One of the classics," Ana said and raised her eyebrows.

"Popular in Monterrey, my homeland," Ricardo commented, looking at Natalia.

"Not so much in Mexico City," said she.

"In your circles, you mean," Ricardo proposed.

"Why do you want to know?" Ana asked, fixing me with a questioning gaze.

"If you allow me to keep tying up loose ends," I started, mimicking Ana's tone of feigned haughtiness, "I remembered that D'Artagnan danced a Jorge Oñate vallenato with Anezka, the woman who would become his wife, at the party that Carlos Cárdenas, alias Rosiñol del Valle, hosted in his apartment in Prague. Oñate is the mnemonic device, a trigger that links a memory to another."

"Well done, you," Ana said and smiled from ear to ear.

You have the memory of an elephant, compadre, Ricardo commented.

"Ana told us the fascinating tale of D'Artagnan, aka Emilio Agudelo in Europe, I'll never forget his name because Agudelo is the last name of a teacher I had in high school..."

"To keep on the topic of memory, the first night we came here, they played that *vallenato*, but without an accordion," Ricardo remarked. "I remember it because I thought it odd, I'd never heard a vallenato without an accordion."

"Another common theme is the decor of this place, of course," I said. "Many years after their first meeting, Cárdenas proposed to D'Artagnan to transform the concept of his bar in the Village from Parisian to Colombian folklore. Fernando, the bartender, told me that Cárdenas came up with the decor for this place."

"The Colombian spacecraft," Ricardo commented and looked up. Above our table hung a traffic signal: a right arrow sign with writing underneath that said, "This Way to Heaven."

At some point, one of the waiters served us a round of shots of *aguardiente*. "From the house," he said, looking towards the bar where Fernando gave us another thumbs up. I raised my hand to indicate that I appreciated it and mouthed my thanks. Ana asked me what was going on, and I told her that perhaps it was a reward for bringing more customers to the restaurant.

"You shouldn't look a gift horse in the mouth," Ricardo commented and lifted his glass. Ana and I did the same. Natalia put hers aside and toasted with her glass of water.

After downing the shot, Ricardo told us that after Rodrigues' job talk, he asked him about the working conditions at Dubai International University. He said that they were great if you were a visiting professor for a year, but he thought it wise to read what current and former employees posted on recruiting online platforms about the long-term working conditions there. I got the impression that it was his way of saying that it wasn't a good place to work.

Natalia commented that she and Ricardo had spent a couple of days in Dubai on stopovers during their trip to Thailand the semester before. "It seemed like a very nice city, I think I could live there," she added.

"It's a kind of Miami, a shopping paradise with beaches, high-end hotels, and luxury condos," Ricardo said. "I am reading a book on the urban transformation of the city written by a British academic. Up until now, it's a typical case of savage capitalism: abundant and extremely cheap labor from poor countries, unfair labor standards, and pretty horrible working conditions." Ricardo was poised to go on but for some reason changed his mind and left it at that.

During the lull in our conversation, I noticed Mr. Windsor, the owner of Goldfinch Antiques, dining nearby. Sitting to his right was a young brunette who could be the woman who was with Cárdenas the first night I came with Ricardo. The other two people sitting with them were a middle-aged white couple.

At some point, the young brunette looked in my direction, smiled slightly, and then said something to Mr. Windsor, who turned to look at me. As if by reflex, I got up and told my friends that I would be back in a minute.

"It's a pleasure to see you again," Windsor said and shook my hand. By chance, we were talking about Spanish colonial antiquities, he added. Then, he introduced me to his friends: to his left, the young brunette, Carolina Abello, who worked at Altamira Art, and to her right, a Spanish couple who owned a taracea workshop and store in Granada.

"If you ever need any restoration work, I would recommend going to Altamira Art," he said with some emphasis. "I have worked with them for several years, and I can vouch for the quality of their work."

"Thanks," I said, and for some reason, I felt like I was a performer in a play. There was something odd about the scene that didn't quite fit. I couldn't help but notice that the bottle of aged rum on the table was almost empty. It occurred to me that Windsor had had one too many.

"We are at your service," Carolina Abello declared.

"I appreciate it," I said and took a step back. "It's nice to meet you all."

Carolina Abello got up suddenly. "Let me give you our card," she said and she rummaged in her bag, indicating with her eyes that we should go to the bar where there was better light.

"You can phone or come during our business hours," she said in a soft, leisurely tone, offering me a card.

I thanked her and suddenly felt a void in my stomach. Sitting at the bar was the stocky man at the door at Altamira

Art the day I went. He nodded his head, perhaps in greeting or as a way to confirm that I was the person who had asked for Cárdenas.

"I understand that you have a bargueño in need of repair. We could help you at Altamira. How old is it?" she asked.

"From the nineteen thirties."

"I thought it was from the sixteenth century."

"I shook my head and remained silent, unable to find the right words."

"We can help you anyway. Our restorers are quite experienced."

"Is Mr. Cárdenas also a restorer?" I felt emboldened to ask.

"One of the best; he learned from his father who worked for art museums in Bogotá in the nineteen fifties."

"Have you worked with him long?"

"For many years; he is my godfather."

"I see," I said, but I wasn't sure what being a godfather meant in that context. "I understand that he is in Dubai," I said.

"You are very well informed," Carolina commented and looked at the stocky guy, who in turn, was looking at me.

"I have a friend in Dubai who is well-connected in the business world," I lied.

"If you are interested in selling your bargueño, we could get you a good price. We have good clients in Dubai."

"Do you work with Christie's?" I asked.

"We occasionally work with them," Carolina Bello replied. "It's a company that appreciates the value of things, something that in Colombia we still have to learn."

"I don't know what you mean," I said. "I don't live in Colombia. But, in the case of the old bargueños, I understand that there are colonial art museums in Bogotá and perhaps in other cities where I'm sure they have specialized curators, perhaps historians and anthropologists."

Carolina Bello looked at me somewhat impatiently; perhaps she judged me naïve. "Museums consecrate some works," she said, putting her bag on the rustic wooden bar stool that marked the center of the triangle that she, I, and the stocky man-made.

"Perhaps those belonging to the well-to-do, or those made by famous artists, in any case, the selected few. It's ironic that taracea works, which were once considered works of art, are now considered artesanías –handicrafts– an ambiguous category associated with the everyday. Handicrafts are what we have in this restaurant," she remarked and looked up at the ceiling. "Together, all these objects are a representation of Colombia, the *concept* that gets customers to come to this restaurant.

"Do you sell them, I mean the handicrafts?" I asked and glanced at Ana and our friends who were chatting animatedly.

"Of course, we have a warehouse in the basement."

"It's good business," I said, meaning to be ironic. "Do you have plans for the future?"

"Carlos is negotiating the opening of a franchise in Dubai," she replied with a smile. Someone had just taken a picture of her, the flashlight bathed her face for an instant.

THIRTY-TWO

Tía Astrid called me as I was crossing Union Square on my way home. She said she was in Tocaima with Juana Medina and that she had several things to tell me.

"I'm all ears," I said and sat on one of the park benches overlooking the marble arch where I used to meet Dad before going to Netsuko. The May afternoon was sunny and radiant and without an iota of wind. It seemed to me that people came and went with a certain lightness, or perhaps I was the one who saw it that way; my favorite season of the year is summer which was coming soon.

"Aldemar told me that he didn't know your great aunts because they left for California when they were very young," Tía Astrid began. "All she knew was that Inés, the oldest, married a young doctor and military officer from Bogotá, who was awarded a scholarship to do a residency at a Los Angeles hospital in the 1950s. Those were turbulent years in Colombia, as you well know, future professor. When he finished his residency, the same hospital hired him, and thanks to that, he and Inés became citizens of the United States.

"Which allowed the other two sisters to come," I said.

"All three became Californians."

All of a sudden, two guitar players dressed in baroque-style costumes that had been set up by the arch started to play a classical Spanish song that sounded vaguely familiar. Perhaps we had it at home in a vinyl LP; Ana is a fan of guitar music from the Renaissance.

"And do you know their names, where they live, whether they had children?" I asked as I searched for an empty bench on the other side of the park.

"That's all Aldemar knew. But Adriana has been digging in –you don't know how persistent she is– and found out that all three sisters died at the beginning of this century, one of them from heart disease; the others she couldn't find out what of. Inés had two children; Gabriela, the second one had three; Maria, the youngest, had no children; she lived her whole life with Gabriela and helped her raise the kids. Adriana found one of Inés's children, one of your second cousins, named –surprise, surprise– Rafael Ruiz, for some reason he uses his mother's last name, through a business social network. It turns out he owns a company that manufactures and sells taracea furniture, based in San Diego."

"Like Carlos Cárdenas in New York," I said and sat down on an empty bench overlooking the corner where chess players gather.

"The Cárdenas business sounds more like a restoration workshop to me, Francisco," Tía Astrid continued. "Your second cousin's company is a large-scale operation: they have branches in Los Angeles, Miami, and Mexico City. But it's not the kind of Spanish colonial taracea that your great-grandfather made. You have to see the photos on the website. The bargueños they make don't have any marquetry: there are no inlaid bone, tortoiseshell, or precious wood plates. Instead, they have drawings of animals and geometric patterns carved into the wood, like in eighteenth-century Spanish bargueños. I suppose it was a pragmatic decision: you can't get tortoiseshells, hawksbill's turtles are a protected species, same with some precious woods; and working with bone is complicated and time-consuming. The company also works on interior decoration projects, including several luxury hotels, imitating the style of the great colonial haciendas in the Americas. Anyway, it's a modern operation. But, if you ask my opinion, it has nothing to do with taracea."

"We can talk about this some other time, you know I'm a bit orthodox when it comes to art and antiques."

"Whenever you want, Tía" and I laughed to myself. I figured she was with Juana Medina, who would be listening to our conversation. A few moments ago, I realized that Tía Astrid had put me on speakerphone.

"Did Adriana get in touch with Rafael Ruiz, my second cousin?" I asked and noticed that a group of people was gathered around a young African-American guy who played simultaneous chess matches with two of the regular players of that corner of the park.

"They've exchanged emails. Rafael is married but has no children. His wife is German of Iranian descent. They are on Facebook. In the posted photos, Rafael bears a resemblance to your father, although he is bald. Rafael's younger brother, Manuel, works for an airline and lives in Atlanta with his Colombian wife. According to Rafael, his three cousins live in New York; a small world. The oldest, also named Rafael —what an outdated custom using the same names over and over is– works for an insurance company in Manhattan; the next one, I no longer remember his first name, Adriana will send you all the information by email, is either an ophthalmologist or an optometrist in Brooklyn. The third one struggles to make a living, and he is the black sheep of the family, and he's had problems with drugs and alcohol. Rafael who works in insurance has a daughter who is a school teacher. The eye doctor married a Jewish woman, and he has two daughters who are both visual artists. Adriana says you can find all of them in the friend list of the Ruiz family from the L.A. Facebook page."

"Wow. I'm stunned. I'd never imagined I had so many relatives," I exclaimed.

"True that," Tía replied, her tone warm. "Moving on to another topic, do you remember the strange photo of your great-grandfather and his three daughters?"

"I look at it every day, Tía."

"I'll tell you what Adriana told me about the fate of those pieces. After ten years of being in L.A., your great-aunt Inés found out through her younger brother, Rafael Ruiz, your grandfather, that the table that your great-grandfather made was for sale at an antique store in Bogotá. Inés called the store and said she was buying the table and would go by in a few days. Once in front of it, she realized it was in poor shape due to humidity and lack of tender care. Some surfaces were scratched, and the tortoiseshell plates on the thin legs had come off. Inés paid no heed and bought it. Since she had learned the taracea craft from her father, Inés set up a workshop in her garage and made a copy of the table. She used plastic faux tortoiseshell, cow bones, and exotic Californian woods. When she finished, she sold it to a Mexican neighbor, and that's what started the business that her son Rafael, your second cousin, inherited. Who would have known that a lineage of artisans hailing from Andalusia or perhaps further back, from Syria, would end up in sunny California, the land of dreams and endless possibilities?"

"I imagine that the bargueño is the one I have."

"We had already concluded that."

"And the frame?"

"It could be one in Casa de Nariño, the presidential palace. Juana found it in an exhibition catalog. To be sure she has to see it in person. She's got an appointment with one of her colleagues in the presidential palace next week."

"Wow, Tía."

"Wow, you."

"I spoke with Gustavo this morning. He was very lucid. He asked me if you had already started writing the dissertation. I told him that maybe it would be a novel. He made light of it and said that in that case, he hoped it could be turned into a telenovela."

"I've got to go. In a minute, I'll forward an unopened email I found in your father's email account. I came across it by accident. I was looking for some old pictures I sent your dad a while ago that I wanted to show to Adriana. It's something important I rather you read on your own."

"Take care, Francisco. A shower of kisses."

THIRTY-THREE

In the early morning, I had the lucid dream again in which I was in a public square with an equestrian statue, next to a German beer hall, where long ago I had dined with a woman. Aware that the dream was going to vanish at any moment, I looked at the tall building where I lived. Clouds flew fast above it, and a pale moon was hiding behind them. In the window of my apartment, I saw a shadow that moved. It was someone I knew, but I couldn't remember who. I had the strange sensation that he or she was watching me with a vintage spyglass. At that moment, I came out of the dream and found Ana's face looking at me with concern.

"Did you have a nightmare?"

"The dream about the square," I replied.

"You've got to tell Dr. Vartatian. You've had it since you started taking that medication she prescribed."

"I will," I said and stretched my arms.

I opened my laptop, which I had left on my nightstand, and reread the message Tía Astrid sent me.

Ana asked what it was about.

"My aunt discovered in my dad's email a long message from my grandfather, Rafael Ruiz, before his death. My dad never read it. It was dated around the time he was due to return to Colombia. Perhaps he thought it was a business matter and decided to ignore it. I'll read what it says. You won't believe it:

Dear Gustavo. As I was telling you in Paris, the two families were related a long time ago. The Ruiz family of my father, your grandfather, from whom I learned the taracea craft, was poor; and my mother's, the Valenzuelas were a family of wealthy landowners. Unfortunately, my dad didn't get along with that family, even though they were his best clients. They lived in a grand old colonial house in Bogotá and all the furnishings were in taracea, it was a family tradition. When my mother passed away, the patriarch of the Valenzuela family demanded that he pay him a sum that he owed plus an exorbitant amount of accrued interest, my father had no choice but to pay off the debt with the bargueño he had inherited from his father, the twin of the famous Arca de Noé. After the patriarch Valenzuela passed away, your grandmother Francisca inherited it, who in turn gave it to your grandfather Gustavo for the antique store. I told Carlos the story when he was fourteen or fifteen, but I never thought it would affect him so much, and that a decade later he would decide to do what he did. By then, I had returned to Tocaima to my son Aldemar's house. When I found out from my great friend Doctorcé, Manuel Carrizosa that Carlos was in Madrid selling the bargueño, I went looking for him to persuade him to return it. I had recently learned that you, my first-born son, was its rightful owner. I already told you how it all happened. I still can't believe that the Valenzuela lawyer was the only one who knew the whole truth.

"Carlos Cárdenas aka Rosiñol del Valle is your uncle!" Ana cried out.

"The news hit me like a hammer," I said.

"That in the end, stayed in the family. That your newly found uncle is an adventurer like your great-grandfather was? That the history of your family have many secrets?"

"Yes, all that, I suppose," I replied. "I can't believe it yet. However, the story has another twist. It suggests an interesting and perhaps troublesome kinship."

"I don't know what you're talking about."

"I just read you what my grandfather said about the Valenzuelas."

"The Valenzuelas? I thought you said the Azuelas. Your first-thing-in-the-morning-Spanish isn't doing you any favors." Ana was about to add something but changed her mind. Then she put her hands on her hips and looked at me with a shocked face.

"How do you know they are the same? There must be hundreds of Valenzuelas in Colombia."

"Surely," I said. "But my second cousin's name is Sara Ruiz Valenzuela, a descendant, on her mother's side, of a Valenzuela family of whom it is known with certainty —from DNA testing— to have a distant Jewish ancestor, as is the case of the Valenzuelas from which your aunt Margarita and your *father* descend."

Ana burst out laughing. "So we end up being related?"

"If I'm right, yes," I said. "Apart from comparing the DNA tests, we would need to do a full genealogy. We would be distant relatives, I clarified. Cousins twice or thrice removed, or something like that."

"As are millions of Colombians, if you undertake the making of a family tree at the national level," Ana pointed out.

"Don't tell me you don't want to find out."

"Of course, dear pirate. Lest our kids be born with a pig's tail."

"It wouldn't be fair to them," I said.

"Speaking of fairness, I'm late for my meeting with Vartatian. We'll talk about this with a cool head later. See you at D'Artagnan's at seven."

As Ana closed the door, I was strangely relieved. I was up all night thinking that Ana would take our distant kinship the wrong way. I imagined that she would find it incestuous or something like that. An absurd idea, I realized, in the light of day.

I would start the kinship chart as soon as possible. The family tree my second cousin Sara Ruiz sent would serve as a starting point. To that, I would add Jacobo, Ana's cousin, who traces the other Valenzuela line. Tía Astrid could help with research at the national archives in Bogotá to fill in the gaps. It would not be an easy task. It would be mostly documents from the 18th and 19th centuries. To make it more complicated, the two families were not from Bogotá, and the documents could still be at the local archives. Perhaps Ana and I could go to Colombia in August to do that research.

The DNA tests would not be a problem. I was sure that Ana and Dad would have no objection, but it was unclear whether Ana's dad would agree to it. From what she's told me, he's not an easy man to get along with. It would be interesting if traces of North African DNA were found in someone on the Valenzuela side. It could give credibility to Alejandra's conclusion that the old man with the beard and turban in the bargueño's engraving was Al-Zahrawi, also known as Albucasis, the Muslim father of modern surgery. Of course, there could be other explanations, other stories behind the history of the bargueño and the bestiaries. Nothing was ever simple; no line was ever completely straight. Lineages were like the crooked streets in the Village or, in colonial Bogotá: full of odd intersections, detours, and dead ends.

With those ideas still in mind I went to the kitchen. I had to eat something; I felt a little weak, I had not been able to sleep all night. I could not get the image of Carlos Cárdenas, whom I briefly saw at *Tierra Natal* out of my head: a tall man, dressed in black, with a long face and an aquiline nose, which together with his Greek cap gave him an eccentric air, like a character in a noir film. Before I saw him at the restaurant, I had imagined him as Joel Cairo, the slippery character Peter Lorre played in The *Maltese Falcon*, another of Dad's favorite movies, which we used to watch at least twice a year, on his birthday and mine, nearly six months apart.

I opened my laptop's photo archive and looked at the ones D'Artagnan sent me of the meeting two years ago between my grandfather and father in Paris. The Carlos Cárdenas I saw did not look like my grandfather Rafael Ruiz or my father, at least in the photos. It occurred to me that perhaps it was because Cardenas was adept at changing his appearance, at being in costume. He was used to acting like someone else. The Castilian gentleman Rosiñol del Valle, who spoke in a thick Madrid accent and wore an ascot around his throat, stole the bargueño and the bestiary from my father. Or the eccentric Andalusian D'Artagnan met in Prague, sporting a Salvador Dalí mustache and slicked-back dark hair.

While eating a bowl of granola, I thought that Ana was right: in the end, it stayed in the family. Carlos Cárdenas, my newly found uncle had simply been trying to set things right. He was only trying to right a wrong. He wanted to get back what he rightfully thought was his inheritance, part of his identity. Tía Astrid didn't blame him. She didn't say anything; she refrained from making any comment. My grandfather was ashamed that his son had stolen the family's bargueño from a half-brother he didn't know. My grandfather himself did not know of his firstborn until the last year of his life.

It was a sunny morning, the sky was dotted with fluffy white clouds; a light, warm breeze was blowing in the street. I had intended to take the subway but decided I would walk instead to the Met. I needed the peace and quiet of its grand salons and its old works of art. It would take me an hour or so to get there, maybe two. It would be a leisurely walk like the ones Dad and I used to do when I was little. I would have lunch at the only other Japanese restaurant I liked in Manhattan, a narrow long space with an open kitchen, near Times Square, where amid the hubbub of Japanese cooks, they served epic Ramen soups, as Ana says. Then, I would have an espresso at the atrium of the old IBM building on Madison and Fifty-Seven; I love its monumental glass and steel geometry and its interior landscaping with rows of bamboo in planters and metal sculptures.

Once in the museum, I would visit Rembrandt's oil painting of a bearded oriental man wearing a turban, the portrait that Dad jokingly said was of a distinguished ancestor of his family, a fancy of his that could well contain some truth. Then, I would pass through the medieval furniture section, the way to get to the Eighteenth-century Spanish painting room, to the portrait of the child Manuel Osorio Manrique de Zúñiga by Goya with the faraway gaze in which not so long ago I saw myself as a child, and in which I now saw my father in the labyrinth of his early dementia, the flip side of a complicated genetic inheritance, which I could bequeath to my children, should I decide to have any. Afterward, I would sit and admire Brueghel's engraving of the Alchemists' workshop. It would help me reflect on the legacy of my great-grandfather, the artist, botanist, and adventurer...

INDEX

ONE	9
TWO	15
THREE	21
FOUR	27
FIVE	33
SIX	41
SEVEN	47
EIGHT	55
NINE	63
TEN	71
ELEVEN	79
TWELVE	85
THIRTEEN	93
FOURTEEN	103
FIFTEEN	109
SIXTEEN	115
SEVENTEEN	123
EIGHTEEN	129
NINETEEN	137
TWENTY	143

TWENTY ONE	149
TWENTY-TWO	155
TWENTY-THREE	161
TWENTY-FOUR	169
TWENTY-FIVE	175
TWENTY-SIX	183
TWENTY-SEVEN	189
TWENTY-EIGHT	195
TWENTY-NINE	201
THIRTY	209
THIRTY-ONE	217
THIRTY-TWO	225
THIRTY-THREE	231

www.ingramcontent.com/pod-product-compliance
Lightning Source LLC
Chambersburg PA
CBHW010315090526
44586CB00039B/2589